LOST CIVILIZATIONS

THE INCAS

James A. Corrick

LUCENT BOOKS
10911 TECHNOLOGY PLACE
SAN DIEGO, CA 92127

Other titles in the *Lost Civilizations* series include:

The Ancient Egyptians
The Ancient Greeks
The Ancient Romans
The Celts
Empires of Mesopotamia
The Mayans

For Steve and Family

Library of Congress Cataloging-in-Publication Data

Corrick, James A.
The Inca / by James A. Corrick.
p. cm. — (Lost civilizations)
Includes bibliographical references and index.
Summary: Discusses the Incas, their government, politics, religion, military organization, decline, extinction, and legacy.
ISBN 1-56006-850-7 (lib. bdg. : alk. paper)
1. Incas—History—Juvenile literature. 2. Incas—Social life and customs—Juvenile literature. [1. Incas. 2. Indians of South America.] I. Title. II. Lost civilizations (San Diego, Calif.)
F3429 .C875 2002
985'.01—dc21

2001004071

10911 Technology Place, San Diego, CA 92127
Printed in the U.S.A.

CONTENTS

FOREWORD 4

INTRODUCTION 6
The Incan Civilization

CHAPTER ONE 11
Before the Incas

CHAPTER TWO 23
The Rise of the Incas

CHAPTER THREE 34
Emperors, Aristocrats, and Commoners

CHAPTER FOUR 44
Bureaucrats and Taxpayers

CHAPTER FIVE 56
Gods and Priests

CHAPTER SIX 67
Soldiers and Engineers

CHAPTER SEVEN 80
The Fall of the Incas

EPILOGUE 91
The Incan Legacy

NOTES 93
FOR FURTHER READING 96
WORKS CONSULTED 99
INDEX 105
PICTURE CREDITS 111
ABOUT THE AUTHOR 112

FOREWORD

"What marvel is this?" asked the noted eighteenth-century German poet and philosopher, Friedrich Schiller. "O earth . . . what is your lap sending forth? Is there life in the deeps as well? A race yet unknown hiding under the lava?" The "marvel" that excited Schiller was the discovery, in the early 1700s, of two entire ancient Roman cities buried beneath over sixty feet of hardened volcanic ash and lava near the modern city of Naples, on Italy's western coast. "Ancient Pompeii is found again!" Schiller joyfully exclaimed. "And the city of Hercules rises!"

People had known about the existence of long lost civilizations before Schiller's day, of course. Stonehenge, a circle of huge, very ancient stones had stood, silent and mysterious, on a plain in Britain as long as people could remember. And the ruins of temples and other structures erected by the ancient inhabitants of Egypt, Palestine, Greece, and Rome had for untold centuries sprawled in magnificent profusion throughout the Mediterranean world. But when, why, and how were these monuments built? And what were the exact histories and beliefs of the peoples who built them? A few scattered surviving ancient literary texts had provided some partial answers to some of these questions. But not until Pompeii and Herculaneum started to emerge from the ashes did the modern world begin to study and reconstruct lost civilizations in a systematic manner.

Even then, the process was at first slow and uncertain. Pompeii, a bustling, prosperous town of some twenty thousand inhabitants, and the smaller Herculaneum met their doom on August 24, A.D. 79 when the nearby volcano, Mt. Vesuvius, blew its top and literally erased them from the map. For nearly seventeen centuries, their contents, preserved in a massive cocoon of volcanic debris, rested undisturbed. Not until the early eighteenth century did people begin raising statues and other artifacts from the buried cities; and at first this was done in a haphazard, unscientific manner. The diggers, who were seeking art treasures to adorn their gardens and mansions, gave no thought to the historical value of the finds. The sad fact was that at the time no trained experts existed to dig up and study lost civilizations in a proper manner.

This unfortunate situation began to change in 1763. In that year, Johann J. Winckelmann, a German librarian fascinated by antiquities (the name then used for ancient artifacts), began to investigate Pompeii and Herculaneum. Although he made some mistakes and drew some wrong conclusions, Winckelmann laid the initial, crucial groundwork for a new science—archaeology (a term derived from two Greek words meaning "to talk about ancient things." His book, *History of the Art of Antiquity*, became a model for the first generation of archaeologists to follow in their efforts to understand other lost civilizations. "With unerring sensitivity," noted scholar C.W. Ceram explains, "Winckelmann groped toward original insights, and expressed them with such power of language that the cultured European world was carried away by a wave of enthusiasm for the antique ideal. This . . . was of prime importance in shaping the course of archaeology in the following century. It demonstrated means of understanding ancient cultures through their artifacts."

In the two centuries that followed, archaeologists, historians, and other scholars began to piece together the remains of lost civilizations around the world. The glory that was Greece, the grandeur that was Rome, the cradles of human civilization in Egypt's Nile valley and Mesopotamia's Tigris-Euphrates valley, the colorful royal court of ancient China's Han Dynasty, the mysterious stone cities of the Maya and Aztecs in Central America—all of these and many more were revealed in fascinating, often startling, if sometimes incomplete detail by the romantic adventure of archaeological research. This work, which continues, is vital. "Digs are in progress all over the world," says Ceram. "For we need to understand the past five thousand years in order to master the next hundred years."

Each volume in the *Lost Civilizations* series examines the history, works, everyday life, and importance of ancient cultures. The archaeological discoveries and methods used to gather this knowledge are stressed throughout. Where possible, quotes by the ancients themselves, and also by later historians, archaeologists, and other experts support and enliven the text. Primary and secondary sources are carefully documented by footnotes and each volume supplies the reader with an extensive Works Consulted list. These and other research tools afford the reader a thorough understanding of how a civilization that was long lost has once more seen the light of day and begun to reveal its secrets to its captivated modern descendants.

INTRODUCTION

The Incan Civilization

High on a mountain in the Andes of South America sits Machu Picchu. Surrounded by other towering peaks, this abandoned city is a monument to one of the great lost civilizations, the Inca Empire. Although deserted by the Incas four centuries ago, Machu Picchu is in remarkably good shape. Many of its massive stone buildings, constructed of carefully sculpted and fitted stones, still stand. Flat, walled terraces, which provided level ground for growing crops in this up-and-down landscape, march like giant steps up the sides of nearby slopes.

Machu Picchu is one of the many windows through which modern scholars peer at the long-gone Inca Empire. The remains of other Incan cities, tombs, and artifacts provide additional windows, as do written accounts of the Incas left by their Spanish conquerors. Historians and archaeologists use these windows on the past to discover what life was like under the Incas and how these people managed to build, run, and eventually lose their empire. Much is still unclear, but centuries of study have given the modern world an understanding and appreciation of this once great and now lost culture.

The Land of the Four Quarters

The rise of the Inca Empire was explosive. In 1400, the Incas occupied only a valley in the Peruvian Andes, but within a hundred years, they had conquered much of western South America, also known as the Andean region. Then, as suddenly as their empire building began, it ended when the Incas fell victim in 1532 to other conquerors, the Spanish conquistadors.

The Incas called their empire Tahuantinsuyu (sometimes spelled *Tawantinsuyu*), or the Land of the Four Quarters, because it was divided into four main sections. This division reflected the Incan belief that the heavens themselves had four parts. Each of Tahuantinsuyu's sections extended out from the Incan capital city of Cuzco, which in the Incan language meant "navel." According to archaeologist Brian M. Fagan, "Four highways from Cuzco's central plaza divided the kingdom into four *suyu* [quarters], which were themselves linked to the four quarters of the Incan heaven."[1]

At its height, Tahuantinsuyu was a rich, mighty domain that stretched some two thousand miles from what is now southern Colombia to central Chile. Its western border was the Pacific Ocean; much of its eastern border was the Amazon rain forest. In between, it contained the Pacific coastal lands and the slopes and highlands of the Andes.

Out of the Inca Empire would come the modern nations of Bolivia, Peru, and Ecuador, as well as parts of Colombia, Chile, and Argentina. Archaeologist Michael E. Moseley writes:

> On the eve of Columbus' . . . landfall it [the Inca Empire] probably surpassed . . . China and the Ottoman Empire as the largest nation on earth. . . . It was the biggest native state to arise in the western hemisphere, and also the largest empire of antiquity ever to develop south of the equator. . . . No contemporary [present-day] . . . Andean state compares in magnitude or prosperity.[2]

The Incas

Some 10 million people lived within the Inca Empire. They were a mix of more than one hundred ethnic groups, speaking twenty languages. The actual Incas, however, were a mere handful, numbering perhaps as few as forty thousand. They were the aristocrats of the empire, and their leader was the emperor, known as the Inca.

From Cuzco, the Incas kept tight control over the affairs and lives of their millions of subjects. In part, they dominated by providing efficient government. They saw that each person had enough food, decent clothing, and proper housing. They also scheduled necessary community work, such as constructing public buildings and roads, and saw that this work was carried out. Further, the Incas dispensed justice and furnished military protection from hostile neighbors.

Machu Picchu is nestled high in the Andes Mountains, and is still studied by modern scholars.

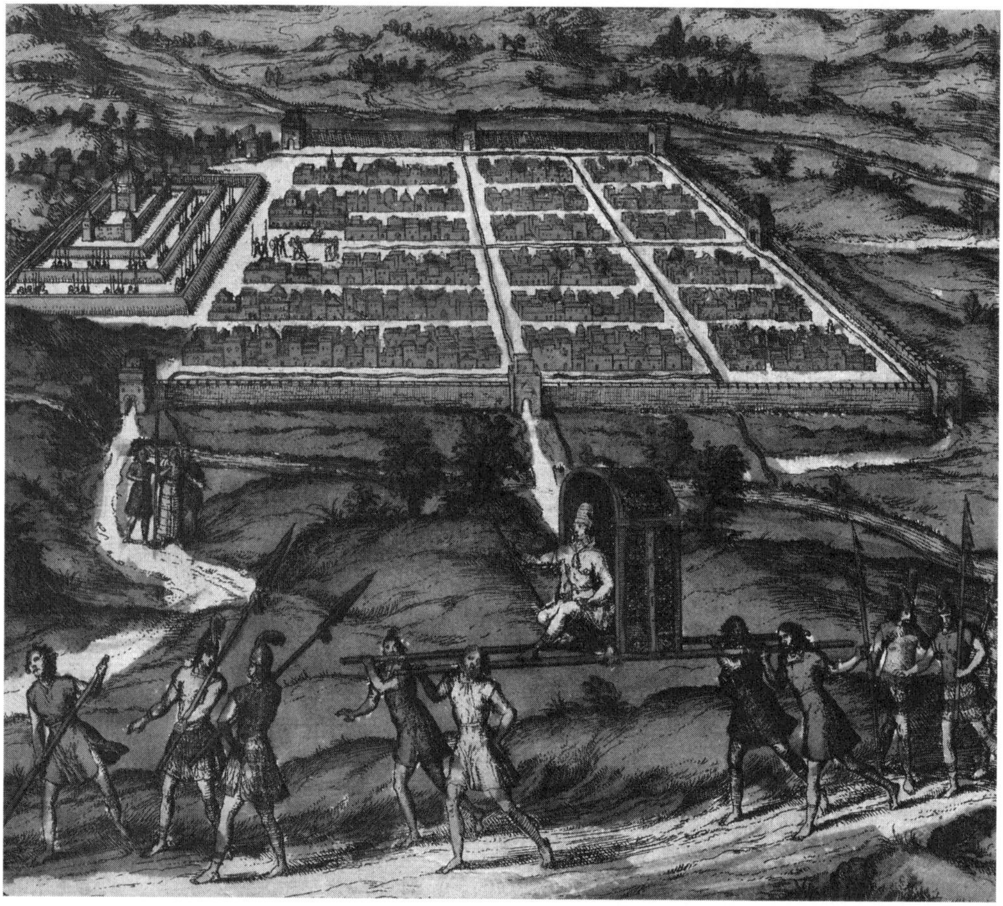

The Incas ruled their many subjects from the capital city of Cuzco. Shown is a rendering of the city.

The Incas also ruled through force. Rebellion was met with swift, deadly military action. The ability of this small group to command the huge imperial population was one of the Incas' greatest accomplishments.

The Incas not only were savvy administrators but also were skilled engineers and talented artisans. They built cities of stone and laid down paved roads that gave them swift access to all parts of their realm. And they produced superior gold and silver work as well as fine textiles.

The Written Record

The Incas did not have writing and thus did not leave any written accounts of their history or way of life. However, they passed down from generation to generation the history of their empire in oral stories and in songs. During the century after the Spanish conquest, a number of Spanish writers collected and wrote down many of these stories and songs. They also interviewed hundreds of Andean natives, many of whom had either lived in the Incan Empire or had parents or grandparents who had lived there.

In addition to these chronicles, other important documents that shed light on Incan history and customs are letters sent home to Spain by European adventurers and settlers. Likewise, Catholic Church and official Spanish colonial records provide useful information about Incan religion and the civic organization of Incan towns and cities. Further, in the colonial records are tax registers that list population figures and occupations of the native people.

The Spanish Viewpoint

The Spanish chronicles and records are rich in detail, but they are not completely reliable. A number of the chronicles were meant to justify the Spanish conquest. In these accounts, the writers portrayed the Incas as harsh and brutal rulers who deserved to be overthrown by the Spanish. Additionally, European missionaries routinely described the Incan religion as evil and corrupt, thus excusing the destruction of Incan holy places and the forced conversion to Christianity of the native people.

None of the Spanish, even such writers as Pedro de Cieza de León, who was sympathetic to the Incas, fully understood Incan society. The Incan world was too different, too alien, from Europe. Thus, the Spanish tended to recast what they heard and saw into a more familiar European framework. For example, Spanish authors mistakenly wrote as though Incan society were based on feudalism, the economic and political system that had begun in Europe during the Middle Ages and was only then ending in Renaissance Spain.

The Incan Viewpoint

The Incas, too, were guilty of historical distortion. As with many people, their official history, which formed the basis for the Spanish chronicles, glorified their own accomplishments while ignoring, downplaying, or denying those of other Andean people. Like the Spanish, they portrayed themselves as benefactors of those they conquered.

In addition, different versions of Incan history existed. One example is the history written by Garcilaso de la Vega, who himself was part Incan, being related to the old Incan imperial family. Garcilaso credited the Incan ruler Viracocha Inca with successfully defending Cuzco from attack by a people known as the Chanca. Most other accounts, however, claim that Viracocha's son, Pachacuti Inca Yupanqui, led that defense.

Archaeology

Through detailed analysis and comparison of the old accounts and records about the Incas, modern historians have been successful in clearing up some of the historical inconsistencies. Further, they have another important

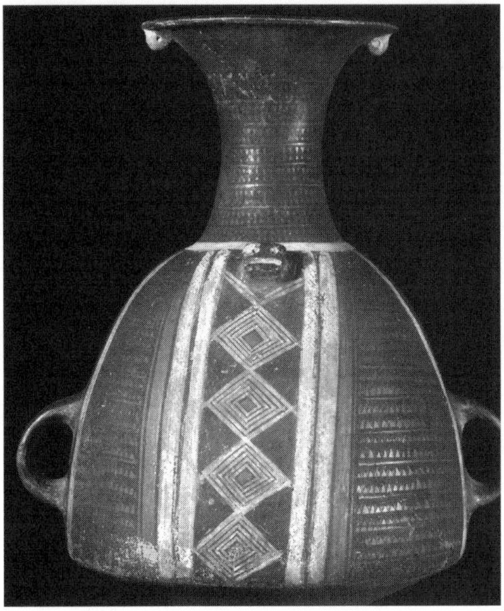

Archeological finds, such as this jar, give insight into the ancient Inca.

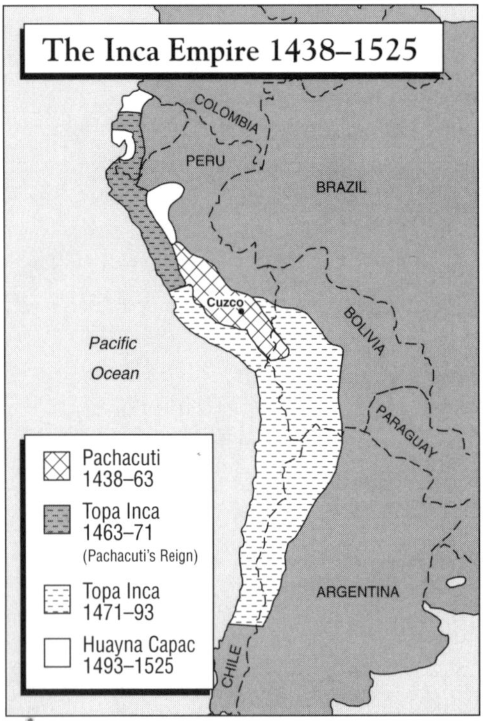

source of information detailing life among the Incas: archaeological studies.

Archaeology pieces together a picture of past cultures by examining their physical remains. These remains include the ruins of houses, cities, and towns; cooking pots, bowls, and other pottery; baskets; and more personal effects, such as jewelry. Archaeologist Michael A. Malpass notes that "the information is . . . different from the kind provided by historical documents, because it provides details about the uses of different sites, the tools they [ancient peoples] used, how their towns were laid out, and where people conducted various activities."[3]

The Incan Archaeological Record

The abandoned city of Machu Picchu is only one of many Incan remains. As the scholar María Rostworowski de Diez Canseco points out, "Through the region once ruled by the Incas, one can find today traces of their urban settlements, sanctuaries, palaces, temples, *tambos* (inns), storehouses, and roads."[4] Portions of these sites have modern cities and towns built over them, but even here, archaeologists can dig down to uncover Incan ruins.

In addition to large structures, many smaller Incan relics have been unearthed. Excavations at Machu Picchu have turned up stone, wooden, and metal tools. Among the richest sources of artifacts are tombs, which can yield elaborately painted and formed pottery, decorated cotton and wool clothing, and finely worked metal jewelry. Food is also found in Incan graves, as are weapons and even toys buried in the tombs of children. Such remains offer some of the clearest views of life during the Incan Empire.

Studying the Present

Historians and archaeologists have one other source for learning about the Incas. They study the customs of the modern native people of western South America. These folk are descendants of the Incas and Incan subjects. They not only still speak Quechua, the Incan language, but also work and live much as their ancestors did. For instance, they string rope bridges across chasms in the same way as their Incan forebearers and use some of the same tools, such as the foot plow, for working the land. They even perform some of the same old Incan rituals.

Scholars have used all the tools at their disposal to recreate the world of the Incas. Although they still have gaps in their knowledge about the Inca Empire and its inhabitants, they have revealed a fascinating and, to the modern eye, exotic society. Yet it was, as modern archaeology has discovered, a society that inherited much from earlier Andean cultures.

Chapter One

Before the Incas

The Incas told the Spanish that theirs was the first Andean civilization and that before their empire, only poorly clothed savages existed in the land. Through the nineteenth century, many scholars took the Incas at their word. Yet there were those who doubted. In 1847, the historian William H. Prescott wrote:

> On the shores of Lake Titicaca [in the Andes] extensive ruins exist . . . , which the Peruvians [Incas] acknowledge to be of older date than . . . the Incas, and to have furnished them with the models of their architecture. . . . We may reasonably conclude that there existed in the country a race advanced in civilization before the time of the Incas.[5]

In fact, the Lake Titicaca culture was only one of many advanced Andean societies existing before the Incas. Beginning in the late nineteenth century, archaeologists, most notably the German Max Uhle and later the Peruvian Julio Tello, showed that many of the sites believed to be Incan were not. Rather, they belonged to other cultures, some of them far older than the Incas. It also became clear that many aspects of Incan technology, Incan art, and even Incan political organization had been invented by these earlier peoples.

The Pacific Desert

Humans began filtering into the Andean region some ten thousand years ago. Archaeologists have dated stone tools found in

Scholar William H. Prescott believed an advanced civilization existed in the Andean region before the Incas.

a cave in the foothills of the Peruvian Andes to 9000 B.C., and a somewhat later date, 8000 B.C., was assigned ancient graves found in northern Peru.

What these early settlers discovered was a hard land of deserts and mountains. Few regions of the world offer the environmental contrasts and challenges of western South America. Of it, archaeologists Craig Morris and Adriana von Hagen write that the Andean region "is . . . notable for its extreme deserts . . . ; cloud forests with almost impenetrable vegetation; and high, windy plains, where daybreak brings summer and nightfall brings winter."[6]

The Pacific coast of South America is one of the driest regions on earth and has been for one hundred thousand years. Little rain falls in this land; some areas go as long as twenty years between rains. It is so dry that even low-water desert plants such as cactus cannot grow there.

A number of rivers, however, run through this arid land from the Andes to the sea, and their banks provide a home to strips of trees and plants. Even so, heavier-than-normal rains in the mountains can cause devastating floods.

Severe earthquakes have been and remain a frequent threat to the region. Also, from time to time, changes in water temperatures in the Pacific affect the climate of South America's west coast.

The Andes

To the east of the desert are the Andes. Stretching the full length of South America, these mountains are a towering, rugged range, with many peaks topping twenty-one thousand feet. Only the tallest mountains of the Himalayas are higher.

The Andes pose their own challenges, such as thin air and steep slopes, where the danger of bad falls and landslides is always present. The range is also a land of ice and fire. Glaciers flow slowly down the sides of many Andean peaks, extending tongues of ice into mountain lakes and rivers. Many active volcanoes are also found in the Andes, and the same geologic forces that give rise to the volcanoes also produce devastating earthquakes.

Yet, there is habitable, fertile ground among these mountains. Many plateaus nestle among the Andes' peaks and contain valleys, lakes, marshes, and flat open plains.

Hunters, Fishers, and Farmers

Despite harsh conditions, by 7500 B.C., people were living in the coastal lowlands and the mountain highlands. Those in the lowlands lived along the rivers, while those in the highlands lived on the plateaus. These early folk were hunter-gatherers. Those living beside the Pacific also fished, for along this barren coast are some of the best fishing grounds in the world.

At first, these groups were nomadic, but by 7000 B.C., many had formed permanent settlements. Agriculture came to both the lowlands and the highlands around 3500 B.C. The rich river bottoms of the desert proved very good for raising beans, squash, peanuts, and corn. An important nonfood crop was cotton.

The highland plateaus also had their farmland. Farming here, however, was difficult. Many of the plateaus, such as the altiplano of Bolivia, are more than two miles above sea level, and even in the summer, night temperatures can drop below freezing. Moseley notes that "few crop types will grow at such heights."[7]

The rugged Andes mountain range is the longest continuous mountain chain on earth. It was home to the ancient Inca Empire.

Frequent drought, hail, and heavier-than-usual frosts meant that good harvests came only once every three or four years. Thus, highland farmers needed cold-resistant plants that could be stored for long periods of time. Among such crops were potatoes and other tubers, as well as some grains. These crops would remain at the heart of Andean agriculture and would play an important role in the later Incan economy.

Guinea Pigs and Llamas

Andean farmers also domesticated animals. One of the earliest of these animals was the guinea pig, which would remain the major source of meat in the region throughout the Inca Empire.

The most important livestock was the llama and its smaller cousin, the alpaca, both distant relatives of the camel. Scholar Ann Kendall comments on the importance of these two animals:

Llamas such as these were valued by the Incan aristocracy for their many uses.

> The llama was the only animal in the Andean region large enough to be used as a pack animal. . . . It could travel about 20 kilometers (12 miles) a day with a load up to 45 kg. (100 lb.). . . . Its wool was coarse but could be used to make cloth-like sacks and plaited [woven] ropes. The alpacas, smaller animals with fine wool, . . . were kept primarily for their fleece. . . . All cameloids [llamas and alpacas] provided meat . . . and leather, as well as other commodities such as [dried] manure for burning.[8]

Herds of these animals would be prized possessions of the Incan emperor and his aristocracy.

The First Cities

About a thousand years after the introduction of agriculture, farmers in the Andean lowlands developed the first irrigation systems. With irrigation, farmers could direct water from rivers and streams to where it was most needed. Also, they could now grow crops in ground that normally never received water.

The result was more food. With more food came an increase in population. More people led to larger settlements that eventually became the first cities. Indeed, the earliest cities in the Americas were Andean. Recent excavations by Ruth Shady Solís at Caral, a site in the Supé River Valley near the coast of central Peru, revealed a city founded around 2600 B.C. It would be another fifteen hundred years before the first urban centers appeared in Mexico.

Caral's population, which numbered in the thousands and which lived in eight residential neighborhoods, became the first large labor force in the Americas. These thousands of workers built a giant earthen pyramid, whose base was the size of four football fields and which rose to a height of sixty feet. Steps cut into its side led up to a flat area, where religious ceremonies were performed. The city also housed several smaller pyramids, which may have been either temples or platforms for the homes of important citizens.

The Andean Cycle of Life and Death

Little is known about life in Caral, since, like all Andean cultures, including the Incas, its people did not possess writing. Yet, they must have been versed in engineering and mathematics to have designed and built the city's pyramids.

Caral had at least two sister cities, perhaps as many as seventeen. All were eventually abandoned for unknown reasons. Possibly, some natural disaster—a flood, an earthquake, or a series of droughts—struck. Such calamities were a fact of life in western South America, and whole societies were sometimes wiped out by them. In any case, Caral and its sisters were replaced by other Andean cultures and cities, which in turn were replaced by still others.

Chavín

Andean societies were fairly isolated from each other, at least until around 900 B.C. when a cultural movement spread throughout much of Peru. Archaeologists name this movement Chavín after Chavín de Huántar, a village located in the central highlands of the Peruvian Andes.

The existence of the Chavín movement was not suspected until 1919 when Peruvian archaeologist Julio Tello stumbled across the remains of a stone temple near Chavín de Huántar. He was impressed with the stonework and began excavating. To his surprise, he found carvings on the stone, as well as painted pottery, similar to those he had seen at a site on the north coast of Peru.

Tello and other archaeologists would later find Chavín work at many other Peruvian sites. These Chavín relics were the first evidence of a unified culture predating the Incas in the Andean region.

Chavín Style

Chavín art had a distinctive style, now called the Chavín style, in which hawks, eagles, jaguars, snakes, and crocodiles were merged with human figures. This style, according to historian Edward P. Lanning, "is an intricate interweaving of mouths, eyes, snakes, and geometric figures . . . in relationships to a central human figure."[9] The animals represent different parts of the human body. Thus, snakes are human hairs, while tails and legs are human tongues.

These half-animal, half-human figures represented supernatural beings. Their importance to Chavín art led scholars to conclude that the focus of the Chavín movement was a primitive religion. As the belief system spread, so did its art.

Chavín de Huántar

Although the region around the village of Chavín de Huántar was important to this early religion, it was not the source of the cult and its art. That source remains unknown. If not the inspiration for the cult, however, the stone temple that Tello dug up at Chavín de Huántar was an important destination for pilgrims, who came from all over Peru. The pilgrims came to hear the voice of the temple's oracle. This voice was the noise of water rushing through canals dug under the building. A maze of stone corridors and galleries within the temple magnified the sound.

The temple was surrounded by a large city, and in addition to pilgrims, traders and merchants also came to the city. Chavín de Huántar was a commercial and cultural crossroads of the Andes. But when the religion lost its popularity around 200 B.C., Chavín de Huántar and Chavín art faded into obscurity.

The Artisans of Chavín de Huántar

Yet before the city vanished, it left an important legacy to Andean, and eventually Incan, culture: the craft specialist. Chavín

Chavín Relics

Archaeologists see the presence of Chavín-style artifacts at many ancient sites in Peru as evidence that the Chavín cult was widespread. In *Art of the Andes*, art historian Rebecca Stone-Miller examines some of the finds at these sites.

> The Chavín style was . . . expressed . . . in all media . . . , ceramic vessels . . . , exotic cut shells . . . , obsidian (volcanic glass) . . . , weaving tools, . . . and . . . gold. . . .
>
> Chavín-style goldwork is known . . . as Chongoyape for the far North [Peruvian] Coast site where a wealth of beaten gold objects were cached [hidden]. . . . Gold sheets were worked into tall cylinders, probably crowns. . . . Gold objects were almost all headgear, face masks, . . . or appliqués on [designs applied to] clothing. . . . Faces are incorporated into this wearable gold art. . . . [A] face has the characteristic upturned fanged mouth . . . and a . . . pair of snakes as the . . . jaw. . . .
>
> Textiles in the Chavín style are known from the burials at Karawa, . . . a South Coast . . . site. They recreate in . . . portable form . . . paintings resembling closely the . . . sculptures of Chavín de Huantar. . . . The Karawa textiles . . . were painted in shades of brown and rose dye on plain woven cotton cloths. . . . Some were sewn together to form very large pieces, one in order to represent a circle of jaguars. . . . Other Karawa textiles include belts . . . and cloths decorated with staffbearing figures. . . . Karawa textiles illustrate many female figures. . . .
>
> Chavín-style ceramics were widely distributed along the coast, . . . [sharing] certain basic characteristics: particularly the . . . spout . . . , in which a cylindrical upright spout splits into two curved ones joining a . . . [globe-shaped] vessel. . . . Vessel bodies feature. . . standing jaguars, seated humans, plants or fruits, as well as . . . double-headed fanged snakes. . . . Chavín-style ceramics epitomize [represent] elegance and power.

de Huántar was the home of some of the earliest artisans who were able to devote themselves full-time to making tools, pottery, clothing, and jewelry.

Among other work, these professional artisans produced some of the finest Andean textiles. They wove cotton and wool cloth on looms of a design still used in the Andes today. Each loom had two sticks, between which ran parallel lines of yarn. Wooden tools were then used to thread other yarn at right angles through these lines. The resulting cloth was often embroidered or painted with geometric designs or with the figures of animals or gods. Indeed, it was the Chavín weavers who developed and popularized painted fabric. All later Andean societies prized elaborate fashioned textiles, often above gold and silver jewelry.

The ability of these artisans to work full-time on their craft was, archaeologists believe, because once more farming methods had improved and so had food production. The result was that a portion of the working population could spend its time on nonfood labor. Malpass observes that "although craft specialization may have occurred earlier . . . , the quality of the Chavín artifacts argues that it became much more developed during this time. Such a development required even more food to be produced by the farmers and herders."[10]

Many fine Paracas artifacts, such as this mummy cloth, were found in ancient cemeteries.

After Chavín

Following the collapse of the Chavín movement, the Andean region saw a number of other cultures flourish and then fade. On the southern coast of Peru, the Paracas (300 B.C. to A.D. 200) was rich in goods, which included embroidered alpaca wool garments, painted pottery, and jewelry. This society also practiced brain surgery. Fluid sometimes collects inside the skull after head injuries and presses on the brain. To drain this liquid, Paracas surgeons either drilled holes in the skull or removed pieces of bone. Such techniques would be used by many other Andean people, including the Incas.

The results of this surgery are seen on over half of the four hundred mummies housed in vertical, bottle-shaped tombs in a Paracas cemetery. This cemetery, discovered in 1925 by Julio Tello and now called the Necropolis, also contained many fine Paracas artifacts.

The Nazca (100 B.C. to A.D. 600) also lived on the south coast of Peru and inherited some of the Paracas culture. Around A.D. 250, these people began filling the nearby desert with huge drawings of animals, flowers, straight lines, and geometric shapes. These drawings, known as geoglyphs and made by removing the dark upper soil to reveal a light subsoil, can be viewed only from the air. The purpose of these geoglyphs is unknown. Some archaeologists speculate that they played a role in Nazca religious rites, perhaps as offerings to divinities believed to be looking down from the sky. Many of the lines point to the

Nazca city of Cahuachi, which may have been a ceremonial center for the culture.

Warrior Priests and Artisans

At the same time that the Nazca were operating on Peru's southern coast, the Moche were conquering and ruling several river valleys on the north coast. Here, warrior priests stood at the top of society, over which they exerted tight control. They also supervised the construction of pyramid-shaped burial mounds, in which they were eventually laid to rest along with their amassed treasures of gold, silver, and copper. In more peaceful pursuits, a whole class of Moche artisans produced the finest pottery and jewelry at any time in Andean history.

Learning about Moche Society

Peruvian archaeologist Luis G. Lumbreras, in his *Peoples and Cultures of Ancient Peru*, shows how scholars use painted ceramics and other relics to understand the society of the pre-Incan Moche, particularly its class structure.

> Some pottery vessels bear hunting scenes in which richly attired "lords" are surrounded by numerous "beaters" [servants] with dogs, while others depict elaborately dressed personages being carried on litters [covered platforms]. Individuals performing menial [lowly] tasks generally are nude or wear only a loincloth or shorts. . . . These servants may really have been slaves . . . , suggested not only by scenes in which they form a line followed by individuals brandishing whips, but also by burials . . . , which were accompanied by . . . sculptures, often of wood, representing nude men with a rope around their neck and their hands tied behind their back. . . .
>
> Status differences were clearly indicated by dress. Men in general wore a loincloth and a short sleeveless shirt beneath a tunic [shirt], which . . . was fastened around the waist by a colorful woven belt. More important persons completed their costumes by adding a large mantle [robe]. . . . The head was always covered. . . . Most common was a turban consisting of fine multi-colored bands wound around a small cap and held in place by a strip of cloth that passed over the top and was tied under the chin. . . . Another typical headdress, which was certainly restricted to important persons, was made from the skin of an animal, whose head protruded at the front. . . . The costume was completed with a great variety of ornamentation, ranging from painting of the skin to jewelry worn on all parts of the body.

The capital city of Moche was dominated by two facing pyramids, the Temples of the Sun and of the Moon. Made of sun-baked bricks, or adobe, the Temple of the Sun rose to a height of 130 feet and rested on a base a quarter mile long. Both temples had murals on their walls showing the beheading of prisoners of war as part of religious ceremonies.

Additional details of Moche life were painted on pottery. It is through these paintings that archaeologists, beginning with Max Uhle in 1899, learned more about this society than has been discovered about most other pre-Incan cultures.

Around A.D. 800, the Moche, like many other Andean civilizations, simply vanished. Scholars speculate that severe drought and earthquake may have brought the warrior priests down. The final blow, however, was by human hands, for the last stronghold of the Moche was burned out, perhaps by an invading army, perhaps by a rebelling population.

Archeologists have learned much about the Moche society through its pottery. This piece features a man wearing a bird headdress.

Highland Civilization

At the height of Nazca and Moche dominance of the coastal lowlands, two advanced societies, Tiwanaku and Huari, arose in the Peruvian Andes. Beginning in A.D. 500, these two would become and remain for centuries the most important highland civilizations. Additionally, Tiwanaku would inspire the Incas to build large stone structures, while Huari would give them much that was Incan, from political organization to roads.

Tiwanaku was a large city-state located on the shores of Lake Titicaca, not far from present-day La Paz, Bolivia. The nineteenth-century historian William H. Prescott was referring to this city when he published his striking theory that the ruins on Titicaca predated the Incan civilization. Tiwanaku's site had been inhabited for a thousand years, but it was not until around A.D. 350 that a city began to grow on the spot. By the beginning of the sixth century A.D., Tiwanaku housed fifty thousand people.

Tiwanaku relics have been found throughout much of the southern Peruvian highlands. However, the Tiwanaku appear to have dominated the region through trade rather than conquest, since most of their artifacts found in other parts of the Andes are standard trade goods—pottery and textiles.

A statue adorns a gateway in the ruins of Tiwanaku.

City of Monuments

The city of Tiwanaku was well planned, and its center was filled with large stone temples, palaces, and statues. Some of the stone pieces were immense and represented much labor in transporting them from quarries and then in erecting and finishing them. In Pedro de Cieza de León's *The Incas*, written in 1553, the Spanish chronicler describes a visit to the city:

> Tiahuanacu [Tiwanaku] . . . is famous for its great buildings, which . . . are a remarkable thing to behold. Near the main dwelling [city] is a man-made hill, built on great stone foundations. Beyond this hill are two stone idols of human size and shape, with the features beautifully carved. . . . Close by . . . , there is another building . . . [with] a finely built wall. . . . Some of the stones are . . . so large that one wonders how human hands could have brought them to where they now stand. . . . There are many large gates with jambs, thresholds, and doors all [made] of a single stone.[11]

The man-made hill Cieza mentions was an actual hill turned into a pyramid by the addition of five stone terraces. It faced a grid of streets lined with large stone buildings. Although the Tiwanaku erected these buildings centuries apart, they planned and designed so well that the structures all appeared to have been constructed at the same time.

A century before Cieza's visit to Tiwanaku, the Incan emperor Pachacuti Inca Yupanqui had been as impressed as the Spanish writer with the monumental ruins of Tiwanaku. He would return to his home of Cuzco and begin rebuilding the Incan capital in stone.

The Conquerors

Where Tiwanaku influenced through commerce, Huari, the other dominant highland culture, controlled through force. Huari's armies conquered much of northern and central Peru's mountain plateaus. The Huari domain even included a portion of the Peruvian coast, although they remained primarily a highland power.

What Huari's relationship was to Tiwanaku is unknown. All that is certain is that both shared a similar style of pottery. Painted ceramics from both cultures show a man with outstretched arms, holding staffs in each hand. Kneeling and running around the human are winged figures. The Huari, however, added a woman to their pottery. Such Andean paintings are often of supernatural beings, and some scholars see the similar pottery design as evidence that Huari and Tiwanaku shared the same beliefs.

Huari Management

From their capital city of Huari, set in the center of the Peruvian Andes, the Huari established a series of military installations throughout their conquered land. They also divided their realm into sections, each of which had its own administrative center.

One of these divisions included the Cuzco Valley, homeland of the Incas. Rostworowski explains:

> There was a city to the south of Cusco [*sic*] . . . , which served as the Wari [Huari] administrative center for the region. This Wari presence must have influenced many aspects of Inca development, including models of organization and of exercise of power. In addition, it appears likely that myths and accounts from that period persisted until Inca times; a few centuries are not a barrier to the preservation of oral accounts.[12]

And indeed, accounts of what the Huari did and how they operated may well have come down to the early rulers of the Inca Empire. For like the Huari domain, the Incan would also be divided into sections, each managed from its own administrative city.

Mountain Terraces

The Huari may also have been responsible for the Incas' use of terraces for growing crops and for the Incan road system. The land around the city of Huari is mountainous, and level ground is at a premium. To give themselves additional farmland, the Huari built

Stone terraces like these allowed the Huari to farm high in the mountains.

stone walls at intervals up and down the sides of nearby mountains. Then they filled in the area behind the walls with topsoil, which was watered by irrigation. Such terraces can still be seen in the Cuzco Valley and at the Incan city of Machu Picchu.

One of the main crops that the Huari grew on their terraces was corn, which could be dried and stored for years. In times of crop failures, Huari authorities passed out this dried corn to the hungry populace. The Incas would have exactly the same corn storage program several centuries later.

Huari Roads

The Huari may also have built a smaller version of the road system that tied together the Inca Empire. Peruvian archaeologist Luis G. Lumbreras writes that "the routes followed by some of the . . . roads . . . suggest that they date from Wari [Huari] times. . . . Many . . . roads lead directly to Wari centers."[13] Lumbreras adds that some of the Spanish chronicles speak briefly about the Incas lengthening and restoring roads that they did not build.

The end, as it had for so many other Andean societies, came abruptly for both Huari and Tiwanaku. Around A.D. 900, the Huari realm broke apart, possibly because of internal rebellion. Tiwanaku hung on for another hundred years, but then it, too, ended. Archaeologists believe that it fell victim to a very long drought. The highland stage was now cleared for the appearance of new power: the Incas.

Chapter Two

The Rise of the Incas

Following the collapse of Tiwanaku and Huari, the highlands became a dangerous place. Constant war was waged between, and even within, cultures as they battled over limited resources—farm and grazing land and water. To protect themselves and their property, whole societies moved to more easily defended locations, and fortresses sprang up across the land. Morris and von Hagen write:

> Archaeological evidence from the highlands suggests that the model of small warring groups . . . was essentially accurate. . . . The resources of the highlands were . . . dispersed. . . . Their [highland people's] economic net had to be cast wide in order to concentrate the quantity and variety of resources needed to support a large-scale, centralized political system.[14]

Like all highlanders, the Incas were also in this contest for resources. The competition would push them out of their valley home and give them the means to create the greatest and largest of the Andean states.

The Chronicles

The Spanish chronicles are virtually the sole source of information about the people and events leading to the creation and expansion of the Inca Empire. Archaeology has a little to add to this part of the Incan story. As archaeologist Duccio Bonavia points out, "Archaeological remains documenting the early development and consolidation [uniting] of the Incas are very scarce."[15] To assign dates to Incan history, scholars still use the time line the Spanish monk Miguel Cabello de Balboa worked out in his *History of Peru*, written in 1586.

Even such a basic question as where the Incas originated remains a mystery. Multiple versions of the story of their legendary first leader, Manco Capac, exist. One account has Manco and his sister traveling from Lake Titicaca to found Cuzco. Another has this first ruler, along with two brothers and two sisters, emerging from a cave near Cuzco. From yet another cave the Inca people are said to have come.

At Cuzco

The details of the Manco Capac legend notwithstanding, the Incas, like many other Andean folk, probably spent years roving the post-Tiwanaku highlands before settling down. According to Cabello, the first Incas arrived in the Cuzco Valley around A.D. 1200. However, many archaeologists believe that the Incas were already in the area by

A.D. 1000 and perhaps earlier. Certainly, excavations have revealed pottery and other relics older than the thirteenth century.

The early Incas lived in a village at a point where three rivers join. The headwaters of a fourth river, the Urubamba, which eventually empties into the Amazon, was just east of the village. These rivers gave the Incas water for their crops and kept the region warmer than it would otherwise be through evaporated moisture that trapped heat from the sun. Still, at two miles above sea level, Cuzco's thin mountain air was often chilly.

Farmers and Raiders

For centuries, the Incas were merely farmers and herders, and nothing set them apart from any other small, closely related band of Andean highlanders. During the 1200s, they slowly spread out to occupy all the available crop and grazing land in Cuzco Valley. However, the center of their culture remained that first village of Cuzco.

The chronicles speak of seven Inca rulers during these early years. Beyond their names, which may indeed be titles rather than personal names, little is known about them. Fagan notes that these "earliest Inca leaders were little more than successful warrior chiefs, based at the growing village of Cuzco."[16]

Loot and Tribute

And successful these warrior chiefs were. Beginning in the early 1300s, the Incas took to raiding their neighbors outside the valley because their homeland alone was not sufficient to feed the Incan population. Thus, whenever they needed more food, they launched a new raid.

Spanish chroniclers wrote of actual armies of six thousand to seven thousand warriors. However, the Incas at this time were still few in number, and consequently, these so-called armies probably ranged from a few dozen to a maximum of a few hundred Inca fighters.

If not driven off by defenders, such Inca bands temporarily occupied neighboring villages or towns while they collected food. As part of their plunder, they also took cloth, pottery, and jewelry. Llamas may have been used to transport this loot, or the Incas may have forced the locals to tote it back to Cuzco for them.

Raids also targeted fortresses, which the Incas routinely destroyed, along with weapons. Such tactics kept the neighboring people militarily weak and at the Incas' mercy. Indeed, by the end of the 1300s, many of the nearby states were paying tribute in the form of food to the Incas, to avoid being attacked.

Beginnings of Empire

Around 1400, the raiders turned into conquerors. Under the leadership of their eighth ruler, Viracocha Inca, the Incas permanently occupied the land surrounding Cuzco Valley, stationing both troops and administrators among their new subjects. This expanded domain was the start of the Inca Empire, and it would remain at the heart of that realm.

Viracocha and his generals had proven themselves to be able military strategists and tacticians. They were the first in a long line of such, who outmaneuvered and outfought their opponents.

Alliance

Viracocha continued his conquests, but soon found himself face-to-face with highland states whose size rivaled that of the In-

Viracocha Inca led the Incas into the land surrounding Cuzco Valley.

cas. To the south were the Lupaca and the Colla, and to the west, the Chanca.

Of the southern rivals, Colla was the greater threat, since it actually bordered the Incan realm, while Lupaca lay south of Colla. Viracocha Inca thus allied himself with the Lupaca, seeking to crush Colla between two converging armies. He forged the alliance by sharing some of the spoils of earlier Inca victories with the Lupaca. In the future, the Incas would routinely offer their allies gifts before war. This practice would become a central part of Incan foreign policy and would create tight bonds between them and many of their allies.

An Incan army marched south while the Lupaca moved north, but before the Incan force arrived, the Lupaca had fought and defeated the Colla. The Incas had a share in the victory feast but not in the plundering of Colla. Nor did the Lupaca allow them to incorporate Colla into the Inca domain.

Colla would eventually recover from its defeat and become troublesome again, although not for many years. The alliance with the Lupaca would eventually break down, but for the moment, with the Lupaca victory, the Incas' southern border was safe.

Invasion

Disposing of the Chanca proved to be more difficult. Around 1438, in Viracocha's old age, the Chanca invaded Incan territory. After fierce battling, the Incas found themselves pushed back to their capital of Cuzco. Convinced that all was lost, Viracocha, as well as his son and heir, Inca Urcon, fled the army and the city.

Another of Viracocha's sons, Inca Yupanqui, however, was determined to save Cuzco. With the aid of Incan allies, Yupanqui met the Chanca outside the city in a bloody battle. According to the chronicler Garcilaso de la Vega in his *Royal Commentaries of the Incas and General History of Peru*, written in 1616, Incan legend has it that even the stones on the ground helped fight the invaders: "They [the Incas] shouted aloud that the stones . . . of the plain were being turned into men to fight in the prince's [Yupanqui's] service."[17]

In the end, the Incas and their allies won. They fought two more battles, soundly defeating the Chanca each time and driving them back across the border. To celebrate the supposed role of the stones of Cuzco in the victory, the Incas collected all the rocks and placed them into shrines.

Civil War

Inca Yupanqui now took the throne at Cuzco and also added to his name the title

THE DEFENSE OF CUZCO

An important turning point in Incan history was the successful defense of Cuzco against the Chancas. In *The Incas*, written in 1553, Pedro de Cieza de León retells the story of that crucial battle.

> The Chancas set up their camp near the hill of Karmenka, which overlooks the city. . . . Along the approach to the gates of the city the men of Cuzco had dug deep holes filled with stones, and had covered them over . . . so that those coming that way would fall into them. . . . The Inca Pachacuti sent messengers to Hastu Huallaca [Chancas general] urging him to come to an agreement . . . to avoid killing people. Hastu Huallaca . . . refused to accept anything but the fortunes of war. . . .
>
> The city of Cuzco is situated among hills in a naturally fortified spot, and the slopes and the base of the mountains had been cleared, and in many places sharp spikes of . . . palm had been set which are strong as iron and more harmful and poisonous. . . . Those of the city . . . [guarded] it on all sides so that the enemy could not enter, for neither Cuzco nor other places in these regions are walled.
>
> When the call to arms was sounded, Hastu Huallaca encouraged his men, urging them to do their utmost, and the Inca Yupanqui did the same. . . . The Chancas bravely came out of their camp, determined to enter the city, and those of Cuzco determined to defend themselves, and . . . many were killed on both sides. But the bravery of Inca Pachacuti was so great that he triumphed over the Chancas, killing them all, so that only a few more than five hundred managed to escape, among these their captain Hastu Huallaca, who, with great difficulty, returned with them to his province.

Pachacuti, meaning "he who remakes the world." Meanwhile, his father and brother set up a rival imperial court at the Incan town of Calca, east of Cuzco. Then the old ruler died, and Inca Urcon took his place.

Civil war erupted. Yupanqui was the more popular of the two rival emperors, and many Calca supporters defected to join the hero of the Battle of Cuzco. Eventually, the war ended when Inca Urcon was killed in a skirmish with his brother's soldiers.

Conquering Armies

The remainder of Pachacuti Inca Yupanqui's reign was one of spectacular conquest. Good military leadership and hard-fighting troops once more led to Inca victories. An army under two of his sons conquered Colla and Lupaca, ending their independence. With these conquests, the southern part of the empire now included all of Lake Titicaca and the regions around it that had once been under the sway of Tiwanaku.

In the west, an army commanded by Topa Inca Yupanqui, another son, put an end to the Chanca threat forever by conquering that kingdom. Topa Inca then turned his attention to the even more powerful Andean state, the kingdom of Chimú. The Incas had already angered the Chimú when their army had earlier conquered Cajamarca, a Chimú ally.

Pachacuti Inca Yupanqui was a great warrior and ruler of the Inca people.

Chimú

Like the Incas, Chimú was expanding through conquest. But unlike the Incas, this kingdom was located in the lowlands. Its capital, Chan Chan, sat on the Peruvian coast, not far from the old city of Moche. Chimú had inherited much of its culture from the older society. Indeed, *Chimor*, another name for this society, is an ancient word for *Moche*.

Archaeologists have linked Chimú to Moche by more than geography. They have also found pottery in the Chimú region that is similar in style and design to that of the Moche. In sum, Fagan writes:

> Civilization was more than 1,000 years old in the Moche Valley. Chimú inherited ancient traditions of kingship and empire and refined them still further. . . . Their rulers were probably descendants of the once-powerful Moche nobles. . . . [They] invested heavily in an elaborate complex of sunken gardens. . . . [They also built] an enormous network of canals that watered flatlands north and west of the city. Their foresight paid off for many generations and Chan Chan prospered. . . . Many military campaigns expanded the empire . . . , until the lords of Chan Chan controlled more than 700 miles . . . of the north coast.[18]

Chimú was also influenced by the Huari, who did have some dealings with the lowlands. Chimú built large walled compounds much in the manner of the Huari, and surviving Chimú architecture owes more to Huari buildings than to Moche. Finally, like Huari and Tiwanaku, recovered Chimú pottery and textiles often show the figure of a

An artist depicts how the walls of a Chimu palace reveal the influence of Huari architecture.

god with open arms, holding staffs in each hand.

Incan Victory

Chimú was the most dangerous opponent yet faced by the Incas. Topa Inca decided that a successful campaign against the Chimú army required simultaneous attacks from several different directions.

The young general spent weeks positioning his troops. He himself was blocked for a time by mountains to the north before he was able to reach a point from which to launch his attack. After a savage battle, Topa defeated the enemy army and marched on to plunder Chan Chan. He then sent the Chimú king as a prisoner to Cuzco, replacing the monarch with a puppet ruler. As an added bonus to the campaign, the Incan military leader extended the imperial border north to include Quito, in present-day Ecuador.

Remaking a World

In 1471 Pachacuti Inca Yupanqui gave up the throne in favor of Topa Inca Yupanqui. The old emperor left the new ruler in charge of the largest, most powerful Andean state that had ever existed.

The Incan army was unmatched in size and ability. Its ranks were swelled with recruits from the Chanca and other subject people. In the years since the defeat of

Chimú, this Incan force had established imperial control along the coast from Ecuador to central Peru. Thus, the Incas became the only Andean society to dominate both the coastal deserts and the Andes Mountains.

Pachacuti had indeed earned his name of "he who remakes the world." But his success was not just in territorial expansion. Moseley remarks that "Pachacuti invented statecraft and institutions such as the national taxation system, the highway and communication system, and the state's extensive warehousing system."[19] These were some of the most important systems that allowed the Incas to rule such a large domain.

The old Inca, supposedly inspired by seeing the ruins of Tiwanaku, also began the rebuilding of Cuzco, turning what had been a simple

CHAN CHAN, CAPITAL OF CHIMÚ

One of the great Incan victories was the conquest of Chimú, a rich, older coastal society. Archaeologist Karen Wise, in *Lost Cities*, edited by Paul G. Bahn, gives the following account of the Chimú capital, Chan Chan.

> The city walls of Chan Chan encompass [surround] more than 20 sq km [12 square miles] of adobe [sun-dried mud bricks], rammed earth, and cane structures that housed thousands. The center of the city . . . comprised eleven huge rectangular compounds enclosed by thick walls . . . that reached 3 m [9 feet] in height. The compounds . . . may have served as the palaces of the royal rulers of Chimor [Chimú]. [Each new ruler probably built his own palace.]
>
> Most of the compounds are divided into three . . . sectors: a northern section, which included the main entrance . . . , as well as a series of courtyards, storage and administrative areas; a central sector, which may have included the king's residence during his lifetime and which also housed a large T-shaped burial platform that served as his final resting place; and a southern sector that featured a large, shallow walk-in well, as well as structures and . . . shelters or shade areas . . . made of cane.
>
> The inside of the [compounds] . . . is mazelike with long narrow passageways with high adobe walls on either side. . . . Access to the inner . . . [rooms was] restricted to the most privileged elite . . . of Chimor. Here a select few viewed the stored treasure of an empire.
>
> Throughout the city adobe buildings, well built but on a much smaller scale . . . , were inhabited by administrators and other elite residents. Most of the remaining inhabitants of the city, including craftspeople, lived in houses and compounds of irregularly shaped rooms made of cane.

village into a city of stone and gold. He may also have ordered the construction of Machu Picchu, to serve as a royal retreat for him and his family.

Cieza and other Spanish chroniclers write that Pachacuti further launched a five-year agricultural program. Gangs of men leveled hills, rechanneled rivers, and constructed farming terraces at one end of the Cuzco Valley. The end result of this labor was increased food production.

Additionally, Pachacuti invented a state religion, whose chief god was the Sun. He erected the Temple of the Sun in Cuzco and scattered priests and temples throughout the rest of the realm, making it clear that the Incas' empire building was a divine mission.

In the Rain Forest

Even as emperor, Topa Inca continued to lead his armies in conquest. His first campaign after taking the throne targeted the

THE REBUILDING OF CUZCO

Among the many reported achievements of Pachacuti Inca Yupanqui was the conversion of Cuzco from a village of modest huts to a capital city of monumental stone buildings. The sixteenth-century Spanish writer Juan de Betanzos relates the story of the rebuilding in his *Narrative of the Incas*.

> Inca Yupanque [Yupanqui] and . . . the [Incan] lords . . . went around the outskirts of the city. . . . In this area they looked over the hills and places where they might find stone quarries and clay for making the mortar. . . . The Inca and the other lords . . . returned to the city. . . . Inca Yupanque outlined the city and had clay models made just as he planned to have it built. . . . [After he had ordered workers to be assembled, he ordered] some to transport rough stones for the foundation and others to bring the clay. . . . He ordered that all the springs be canalized [channeled] in such a way as to be piped to the houses of the city and to be made into fountains to supply water to the city. . . .
>
> The Inca Yupanque ordered everyone from the city of Cuzco to leave their houses, take out everything they had in them, and go to the small towns nearby. . . . He ordered those houses to be torn down. . . . The Inca with his own hands . . . had a cord brought and measured with the cord the lot and houses that were to be made and their foundations and structures. With all of this prepared, the foundations were dug. . . . While these buildings were being made, the work went on continuously with fifty thousand Indians on the job. From the time that Inca Yupanque ordered the beginning of the improvements . . . , twenty years elapsed.

A temple like the one depicted here was erected in Cuzco for the Inca's chief god, the Sun.

rain forest that lapped the eastern slope of the Peruvian Andes.

Topa had little success here, nor would later Inca military ventures in this region. The terrain and environment were just too alien to the highland natives, who never developed tactics for fighting in thick growth and heavy humidity. Topa, however, was able to establish trade relations with some of the people of the rain forest and, in exchange for some bronze tools, hired a group of local archers for his army.

Rebellion

Topa broke off his rain forest campaign when news reached him that the Lupaca and Colla of the Titicaca district had rebelled. The two once-independent groups had received mistaken word that Topa was dead and had massacred the local Inca garrisons and administrators. Reportedly, the rebel armies ate the dead men.

The emperor was outraged and swore vengeance. Again, he personally led his armies. He first defeated the Colla by taking one by one a series of mountain fortresses to which the rebels had retreated. The victorious Inca army then crushed the Lupaca.

The emperor treated the rebels harshly, a practice that later emperors would also follow. According to Bernabe Cobo in his *History of the Inca Empire*, written in 1653, "He had the two main caciques [chiefs] skinned and he ordered two drums to be made from their hides."[20] The rest of the rebel leaders were beheaded and their heads mounted on spears, while many of the rebel soldiers were taken to Cuzco and sacrificed in the Temple of the Sun to celebrate Topa's victory.

The Final Years

Topa did not long remain in Cuzco. He and his army were soon marching south, where they first conquered the highlands of Bolivia. Then they pushed further south, capturing land in present-day northern Chile and northwestern Argentina.

A year or so later, in 1476, Topa Inca launched his final offensive, this time against the south coast of Peru. Many of the towns and cities meekly surrendered to the Inca army, particularly when promised a share of the riches the empire now possessed. However, a few fought bitterly against the invaders, one group managing to hold out for three years. In the end, the Incas' superior numbers and able leadership won out.

Topa Inca's conquering armies were responsible for giving the Inca Empire most of its territory. Because of the size of these conquests, Michael E. Moseley labels Topa the Alexander the Great of South America.

The emperor spent the last years of his life traveling his realm, taking care of administrative matters and refining the imperial institutions. Among other things, he introduced a labor scheme that distributed the adults of the empire into units that allowed administrators to systematically assign people to work and to the army.

Child Ruler

In 1493 Topa Inca died. Originally, he had named a young son, Huayna Capac, still only a boy, as his heir, but had changed his mind in favor of an older son. An internal palace struggle followed, which Huayna Capac's supporters won. The young boy was placed under a regent, who then tried to seize the throne for his own son. An uncle of Huayna Capac foiled the plot, killing the regent, and the young boy grew to adulthood as emperor.

Huayna Capac's reign was more peaceful than that of his grandfather and father, although he did push the northern border into Colombia. Most of his thirty years as Inca were consumed with the more ordinary matters of running such a huge state and of building Quito into a second capital to oversee affairs in the northern half of the empire.

Inca Huayna Capac reigned during the golden age of the Inca Empire.

The Golden Age

Only two generations old, the Inca Empire was so new that its many peoples and cultures were still undergoing unification. Some scholars believe that the Incas never did fully control their southern conquests in Argentina and Chile. Indeed, it is unlikely that the Incas ever enjoyed as tight a control over the imperial population as they claimed to their Spanish chroniclers. One of Huayna Capac's greatest annoyances was a series of small rebellions that flared up at various points throughout the empire.

Yet, the reality and extent of the Inca Empire is unquestionable. Their relics—pottery, textiles, jewelry, buildings, and roads—are found today in every part of the land they described as their own. Archaeologist Nigel Davies points out that the Spanish accounts "define the Inca realm as stretching from northern Ecuador to central Chile, thus . . . corresponding to the traces of Inca occupation as now identified by archaeologists."[21]

And even if still incomplete, the Inca Empire of Huayna Capac was in its golden age. Its government functioned, its people were fed and sheltered, state religion flourished, and its building of roads and cities went smoothly. It was a working society.

Chapter Three

EMPERORS, ARISTOCRATS, AND COMMONERS

The society over which the Incan emperor Huayna Capac ruled was an ordered one. Everyone had a place, and everyone knew what that place was. The Spanish chronicles present a fairly consistent picture of Incan society. It was a pyramid, with the emperor at its apex, and at the bottom, the common people. In between was the aristocracy. There was little social mobility. One was born into a class and died in that class. Each level of society had its duties and its obligations.

The Ayllu

The basic social unit of the Incan Empire, for aristocrats and commoners alike, was the household. The head of each household was male, with the remaining members being the man's wife and children.

Households were collected together into groups called ayllus. The number of households in an ayllu varied, but its members were at least distantly related, the men and many of the women being descended from one or more common ancestors, whose mummified bodies were kept as sacred relics by the ayllu. Moseley observes:

> Common ancestors gave ayllus their ethnic identity, and . . . [leaders] ruled by claiming close blood-ties to founding forefathers. Ayllus were often named after their founders, who were heroic figures, if not mythical ones, and could turn into stone or some special object. They secured lands for their people, established codes of behavior, and were models for proper life. Their corpses were worshipped, and were ranked among the ayllu's most sacred . . . holdings. If outsiders captured these vital relics, the ayllu could be held hostage.[22]

Such ancestor worship was in addition to the official state religion.

An ayllu had its own political and religious leaders, who oversaw the group's affairs and conducted ayllu ceremonies. The Incan ayllus were similar to those found in the Andes today, where individuals serve as political leaders and then religious before retiring from public office.

Marriage

Among other matters, ayllu leaders helped arrange marriages. Normally, marriage partners came from within the same ayllu. Except for the aristocracy, the bride and groom could not come from the same household nor be close relatives. The man was generally twenty-five, and the woman between sixteen and twenty.

The ceremony was simple. The groom and his family arrived at the bride's home, where, to show his acceptance of her, he placed a sandal on her right foot and then grasped her hand. Both families then went to the house of the groom's parents. There the new wife presented her husband with a fine woolen shirt she had made. Finally, after a period of lectures to the newlyweds on how to be proper husband and wife, the families joined the rest of the ayllu for a wedding feast. The newlyweds then moved into a house built for them by the ayllu.

Husbands and Wives

Under Incan law, while women could only have one husband, a man could have more than one wife, but only if he could afford a second or third one. Outside of the aristocracy, few men could. Even those men who had multiple wives had but one principal, or official, wife. The others were secondary wives. Only the principal wife was wed in a ceremony; the secondary wives were merely brought into the household.

No divorce was possible in Incan society between husband and official wife. A man, however, could tell a secondary wife to leave at any time; she, on the other hand, could not leave him.

Royal Household

The emperor's household was its own ayllu and was large, since Incan rulers always had many wives and children. As was customary, the Inca had only one official wife, the *coya*, or empress. Prior to Topa Inca Yupanqui, the emperor normally married a princess of another Andean state, thus forming a political alliance through marriage. However, beginning with Topa Inca, the Inca ruler married one of his full sisters—that is, a sibling with whom he shared the same mother and father.

Manco Capac, the legendary first ruler of the Incas, had supposedly married his sister, and the tradition of incestuous relationships established by Topa created a link between the current Inca leader and Manco.

Royal Ayllus

In addition to the reigning monarch's ayllu, the royal ayllus of all previous emperors still

The emperor is shown here with his wife. Incan rulers often used marriage to form political relationships with other states.

existed. When an Incan monarch died, his body was mummified, and he was treated as though he were still alive. Each of these royal ayllus, as Rostworowski writes, "had the obligation to preserve the mummy of the deceased ruler and guard the memory of his life and achievements by means of songs . . . and paintings passed from generation to generation."[23]

As was usual for nonroyal ayllus, all of a dead emperor's male descendants remained members of his ayllu, with one exception. That exception was the current Inca, who created a new ayllu for himself and his household. At the time the Spanish arrived in Peru, there were eleven royal ayllus.

By custom, the ayllu of a former emperor retained ownership of all the dead ruler's land and the wealth it produced. The living Inca had no access to the property of the former emperors.

Therefore, a new Inca quickly had to find means of supporting his ayllu. Some scholars speculate that this need for income may have been partially responsible for the expansion of the Inca state, with each new monarch adding new lands so as to build his own treasury.

The Unique Inca

In a sense, the empire was a single household, at whose head was the emperor, also known as the Sapa Inca, or the Unique Inca. In theory, all the men in the domain were his sons and all the women his wives.

The emperor's authority rested first on his claim of being a direct descendant of Manco Capac and, second, on his claim of being related to the Sun, the chief deity of the Incan state religion. Thus, the Sapa Inca was divine and ruled by divine right. He was an absolute monarch whose word was law. No one could contradict him; no one could countermand him.

Imperial Presence

The emperor cut an imposing figure, meant to awe his subjects with his might and power. To emphasize his rank, he dressed in the finest wool clothing available. A sleeveless, knee-length tunic covered his upper body while striped trousers covered his legs. A white cloak decorated with geometric designs hung down his back, and he had white wool sandals on his feet. He never wore the same garments twice and often changed his clothes several times a day.

To further indicate his rank, the emperor wore a braided, multicolored headband with a red fringe. From the fringe dangled gold tubes and red tassels. Large earplugs, disks of gold, were placed in holes in each earlobe.

During important ceremonies, the Inca held a long staff made of gold and hung a golden disk that represented the Sun from his neck. He sat either on a throne made of solid gold or on a wooden chair covered with carvings and padded with decorated cloth.

Even the highest-ranking members of society had to humble themselves before the emperor. Scholar Ann Kendall notes that "a person desiring to come into the Sapa Inca's presence, whatever his rank, took off his . . . sandals and put a token burden on his back as a sign of respect."[24] The audience seeker spoke with lowered eyes. The emperor was often seated behind a screen, and if he spoke, his speech was brief. Sometimes he relayed his messages through another person. All of these actions emphasized his remoteness from the rest of humanity.

Royal Display

The seventeenth-century Jesuit Bernabe Cobo, in his *History of the Inca Empire*, paints a picture of the Incan emperors' life.

> The Incas [emperors] made a majestic display both in their personal style of life and adornment and in the pomp and splendor that accompanied them and with which they were served inside and outside their homes. . . . They were served all the exquisite, precious, and rare things that the land produced. . . .
>
> The king ate while seated on a small stool. . . . The table was the ground, as it was for the rest of the Indians, but it was set with great . . . richness, including . . . sumptuous [lavish] food. . . . Serving women brought him all his food on gold, silver, and pottery plates and set them before him on some very thin, small green rushes [reeds]. When he pointed out the dish that he wanted, . . . one of the . . . women would take it to him and hold it in her hand while he ate. . . . All leftovers from the meal and whatever the Inca touched with his hands were kept by the Indians in . . . chests . . . ; thus in one chest they kept the little rushes . . . ; in another, the bones of the poultry and meat left over from his meals. . . . Everything . . . was kept in a . . . hut . . . that an important Indian had charge of, and on a certain day each year it was all burned.
>
> Wherever he went, . . . the Inca was carried on the shoulders of bearers supporting a splendid litter. . . . When the Inca traveled, he had a large following. . . . The Inca also showed his majesty by traveling slowly . . . , and wherever he stopped, accommodations [lodgings] were prepared for him as elaborately as if he were in his court.

Imperial Succession

Unlike a European ruler whose firstborn, legitimate son was automatically his heir, the Sapa Inca might choose any one of the sons of his official wife as heir, not necessarily the oldest. The Incan emperor selected the son he thought most capable of ruling the empire. Sons of his secondary wives were barred from succession.

Incest, as practiced by the Inca emperors, eventually produces children with below-normal intelligence, as well as other mental and physical problems. However, since imperial incestuous marriage was a custom for only a short time among the Sapa Incas, being first practiced by Topa Inca, these problems had yet to appear. At least, no record of them exists in the Spanish chronicles.

There was often a trial period when the heir shared the imperial duties with his father. If the designated heir failed to perform

ENTERING ADULTHOOD

Boys of the Incan nobility had to undergo a series of trials before being admitted to adulthood. The Spanish chronicler Garcilaso de la Vega, whose mother was Incan, describes part of this testing in his *Royal Commentaries of the Incas and General History of Peru*, written in 1616.

> The candidates were required to observe a very strict fast for six days, receiving only a handful of raw *sara* (their corn) apiece and a jug of plain water. . . . Such a rigorous fast was not usually permitted for more than three days, but this period was doubled . . . , in order to show if . . . [the candidates could] suffer any hunger or thirst which they might be exposed to in time of war. . . . Anyone who showed weakness . . . or asked for more food . . . failed. . . . After the fast they were allowed some victuals [food] . . . and then . . . made to run from the hill called Huanacauri . . . to the city, . . . a distance of . . . a league and a half [five miles]. . . . Whoever reached [the finish] . . . first was elected captain over the rest. Those who arrived second . . . and down to tenth fastest were also held in great honor, while those who flagged [faltered] or fainted . . . were disgraced and eliminated. . . .
>
> The next day they were divided into two equal bands. One group was bidden to remain in [a fort] . . . , while the other sallied forth [left]. They were required to fight . . . , the second group to conquer the fort and the first defending it. After fighting . . . for the whole day, they changed sides on the morrow [the next day]. . . . In such struggles the weapons were blunted . . . ; nevertheless there were . . . casualties which were sometimes fatal, for the will to win excited them to the point of killing one another.

well or lost favor for some other reason, he would be replaced by another son. This practice was a source of friction among the potential heirs and often led to palace intrigues and civil war upon an emperor's death.

Incas-by-Blood and Incas-by-Privilege

Directly below the emperor on the social pyramid were the rest of the Incas. Only members of the Quechua-speaking groups living in and around Cuzco Valley were Incas. All of the remaining peoples of the empire were Incan subjects. The Spanish failed to understand this difference and called any Andean native Incan or Peruvian.

Among the Incas, there were two classes: Incas-by-blood and Incas-by-privilege. Incas-by-blood were either relatives of the emperor or members of the valley population, although not related to the imperial family. Incas-by-privilege belonged to groups living near the Cuzco Valley.

All Incas, whether by blood or privilege, were part of the imperial aristocracy, although the former were of higher rank. "Their position," Davies writes, "was unassailable and immutable [unchanging]. . . . [They] were exempt from taxes. . . . They were supported by the king [Sapa Inca] through his revenues."[25]

Incas had many special privileges. They had the right to wear a headband, although it lacked the red fringe of the Sapa Inca. Also, the aristocracy wore earplugs, somewhat smaller than those of the emperor. And as with the monarch, an Incan aristocrat had several wives. For his official wife, he could choose one of his father's daughters, as long as she was not also a daughter of his own mother. Moreover, the aristocracy was allowed to own luxury goods. They wore fine clothing, ate off gold and silver plates, soled their sandals in silver, and carpeted their homes with wool tapestries. So they might have the time to enjoy their luxury, they were permitted servants to tend to their houses and land.

Working Aristocracy

Rich they might be, but Incan nobles were not idle. They served at the highest levels of the imperial government. They also were the generals and senior officers of the empire's army. And they formed the priesthood.

Helping the Incan aristocracy in these duties were the officials called *curacas*. They were non-Incas who made up the third tier of Incan society. They were either local leaders of a subject people or recruits from those folk with a gift for management. The *curacas* formed a secondary aristocracy, receiving some of the same privileges as the Incan nobility.

Training and Testing

To ensure that the nobles would be able to perform their duties, the sons of both Incan aristocrats and *curacas* went to school in Cuzco. For four years, beginning around the age of twelve, they listened to lessons in Quechua, religion, history, geometry, and astronomy, as well as learned about poetry and music. Discipline was maintained by ten strokes of a rod across the bottom of the feet. Such beatings were limited to one per day.

At age fourteen, the young nobles underwent a series of tests of strength, endurance, and courage. They undoubtedly received training, particularly in the use of weapons, throughout their childhood, but its extent and nature are unknown.

After religious ceremonies, the boys raced each other to the top of a nearby hill, showed their skill with slings and bows, and fought each other in mock battles. Then they had to stand sentry duty for several nights in a row without sleep. Next they silently bore hard punches to the shoulders and remained stock-still without flinching while an army officer swung a club above and alongside their heads. The officer then threatened their eyes with a spear. Finally, each young man made a bow, a sling, and a pair of sandals.

In a final ceremony, the emperor pierced the young aristocrats' ears with a gold pin and gave each a set of gold earplugs. Upon returning to Cuzco, relatives gave the young nobles gifts, which included weapons, and lectures on how they should conduct themselves in the service of the emperor.

The Commoners

At the bottom of Incan society were the common people, who made up the bulk of the imperial population. These folk were all members of cultures conquered by the Incas. They were the empire's farmers, laborers, servants, ordinary soldiers, and even skilled artisans.

Commoners led a very restricted life. They were forbidden to possess anything more than was absolutely necessary to meet their basic needs: plain clothing, cooking gear, and tools. All other items were considered luxury goods that only the royal family, the Incan aristocracy, and the *curacas* could possess.

Commoners were also denied education. The extent of their knowledge was what

A manuscript page depicts a taclla or "foot plow" that was used to churn soil and plant seeds.

they learned from parents and ayllu members. The imperial position on education for common folk was summed up by one Incan ruler, who said, "It is not right that the children of the plebeians [commoners] should be taught knowledge . . . , lest the lower classes rise up and grow arrogant and bring down the republic [empire]: it is enough that they learn the trades of their fathers."[26]

Workforce

The commoners supplied all the labor that was needed by the empire, and since the Incas had no machines, all that work was by hand. The Incas did not even have animals large enough to drag loads or pull plows.

For example, commoners used hand tools to work the mines, which produced copper, silver, and gold. Mine shafts were dug into the ground or driven into mountain rock faces, depending on where traces of metals were spotted. Digging was done by scraping the dirt away with wooden or bone trowels. Rock was penetrated by first heating the stone until it cracked. Then workers pushed wooden wedges into the cracks and, swinging stone hammers, drove the wedges deep until part of the rock face crumbled away. In this slow, laborious way, the miners dug tunnels, some of which stretched over 250 feet in length. The excavated dirt or rock, after being checked for precious metals, was carried off in llama-hide sacks by other workers.

A commoner's major task, however, was farming. As the following description by Lanning shows, this work was also hard, physical labor:

> An important Incan invention was the *taclla* or "foot plow," a long pole with a bronze point, a foot rest, and a handle. . . . It permitted the soil to be

GOLD MINES

In his *An Account of the Conquest of Peru*, written in 1534, the Spanish soldier Pedro Sancho provides an eyewitness account of Inca gold mining, reprinted in Ann Kendall's *Everyday Life of the Incas*.

> The mines are in the gorge of a river about half-way up the sides. They are made like caves, . . . whose mouths [were made by scraping] the earth . . . with the horns of deer and [the dirt] was then carried outside in certain hides sewn into the forms of sacks [of llama hide]. . . . The manner in which they wash the earth [to reveal gold] is, they take . . . water from the river, and on the bank they set up certain very smooth flag-stones on which they throw water . . . and the water carries off the earth little by little so that the gold is left upon the flagstones. . . . The mines go far into the earth. . . . A great mine which is called Huayna Capac goes into the earth some 80 meters [260 feet]. They [the mine shafts] have no light, nor are they broader than is necessary for one person to enter crouching down, and until the man who is in the mine comes out, no other can go in. . . . At night when they return to their houses in the village, they enter by a gate where the overseers . . . [receive] from each person . . . the gold that he has got. There are other mines . . . scattered about through the land, which are like wells, a man's height in depth, so that the worker can just throw the earth from below on top of the ground.

> turned as with a plow rather than simply perforated [dug full of holes] for the planting of seeds. A line of men worked across the field, driving the *tacllas* in, turning up the soil, stepping back a pace, and repeating the process, while a line of women faced them breaking up clods with clubs or hoes. . . . The same techniques are still widely used by Andean Indians today.[27]

The women also picked up any stones the plowing turned up.

Women of the Empire

The usual practice was for commoner women to work the fields with the men. Indeed, a wife was expected to serve her husband in whatever ways he thought fit. This expectation applied to all women regardless of their social rank.

In addition to working the fields, commoner wives carried heavy loads for their husbands. They also were responsible for cooking meals, cleaning the house, and making their family's clothing, doing all the spinning, weaving, and sewing themselves. Of course, they also took care of the children,

THE WEAVERS

Among the Incas, one of the most important duties of married women, aristocrat or common, was weaving. The part-Incan author Garcilaso de la Vega, in his *Royal Commentaries of the Incas and General History of Peru,* written in 1616, details this domestic chore.

> [Incan women] busied themselves with spinning and weaving wool in the cold districts and cotton in the hot. Each woman spun and wove for herself, and for her husband and children. They sewed very little for the garments worn by both sexes required very little sewing. . . . Every piece of cloth that they made . . . was made with four selvages [borders]. Cloth was never woven longer than was needed for a single blanket or tunic [shirt]. Each garment was not cut but made in a piece, as the cloth came from the loom. . . .
>
> The Indian women were so fond of spinning and so reluctant to waste even a short time that as they came or went from the villages to the city or even one quarter [house] to another, visiting one another . . . , they carried equipment for the two operations of spinning and twisting [threads of yarn together]. As they walked along, they twisted what they had spun, this being the easier task. While visiting they would take out their distaff [wool-holding rod] and spin as they conversed. Spinning and twisting on the road was done by the common people, but . . . [those] of the royal blood were accompanied by servants carrying their yarn and distaffs. Thus both the callers and ladies of the house were occupied and not idle while they conversed. . . . The quantity that they spin is little, because the operation is a lengthy and complicated one.

Incan women spent much of their time weaving cloths like this one.

carrying their babies on their backs while they worked.

Imperial inspectors made regular visits to check on the conditions of each household. They were always interested in seeing how clean a house was and how sanitary was the food preparation. They also checked on how well the children were being raised, whether the young ones knew their place in society and what their obligations to the emperor and the empire were.

Aristocratic Women

According to Malpass, royal and noble women had a much easier life:

> The lives of noble women were no doubt easier than those of commoners; they had yanaconas [servants] to tend to many of the duties assigned to women. Yet fundamental activities such as spinning and weaving were conducted by all women, of high class or low. Principal wives were in charge of running the household and delegating duties to the secondary wives. Their task was more managerial: making sure that the household ran smoothly and that food and drink were prepared to high standards when important individuals were entertained. It probably fell to the secondary wives to do the preparations.[28]

In large households, each son of the principal wife was given one of the secondary wives as his nanny, who bathed and in general cared for the boy until puberty. At puberty, she instructed him in sex, and when he married, she went with him to his new home.

Influential Women

Most women were relatively powerless in Incan society, but not all. According to Bernabe Cobo in his *History of the Inca Empire*, written in 1563, some women controlled land and herds. Others were religious leaders, being priestesses of the Moon and other female deities.

Moreover, empresses often swayed their husbands' thinking, thus influencing imperial policies indirectly. Some even played a more active role. Pachacuti Inca's empress, for instance, ruled Cuzco when he was away, even supervising disaster relief after one violent earthquake, while Topa Inca's principal wife concluded a treaty with the city of Yanayacu.

In general, both women and men were locked tightly into their place within Incan society. It was a society that valued and promoted control because it enabled a single ruler, operating through a small elite, to manage and run the geographically huge and ethnically diverse Inca Empire.

Chapter Four

Bureaucrats and Taxpayers

The Inca Empire was wealthy. It had storehouses full of food, clothing, and other goods; its aristocratic homes were full of luxuries. No one wanted; no one begged for food. Efficient management of the economy was the source of the imperial riches. Commands and authority flowed easily and naturally from the top, the emperor, through the layers of bureaucrats, members of the nobility, down to the common people.

Incan Economy

The Incas had a moneyless economy: They had no coins or any other form of currency. Instead, they had what scholars call reciprocity—that is, goods were exchanged for work or vice versa. When the emperor wished to reward imperial officials or army officers for serving the empire, he gave them jewelry, fine textiles, weapons, livestock, land, and even women to be secondary wives. Commoners, working on government projects, received food and clothing.

Three valuable resources—land, livestock, and labor—formed the foundation of the imperial economy. Rostworowski observes that "the yield created through the exploitation of these resources was translated into consumable goods, which were stored in warehouses and represented the state's assets."[29]

Land

Private land ownership was rare in the Inca Empire. In the Cuzco Valley, the royal ayllus and some Incas-by-privilege owned farms and country estates.

Most land in the empire, however, belonged to the emperor, who allowed much of it to be used by others. The Sapa Inca di-

The emperor rewards his subjects with gifts for serving the empire. Money was not used by the Incas.

vided his land into thirds. Part was reserved for the Incan state, part for various temples, and part for the local ayllus. Those sections of land reserved for the use of temple and ayllu could neither be sold nor traded.

Each ayllu parceled out its land among its households, with every household head being assigned a tract that was large enough to support him and his family. Archaeologist Louis Baudin notes that these tracts were not equal in size:

> Each family received . . . a plot of ground which should be sufficient for sustaining life. . . . This plot varied according to the quality of the soil, which is logical. With the birth of each son a supplementary [extra] plot was allocated [given] to the parent, and with the birth of each daughter a half plot.[30]

Along with the land went control of water sources, such as springs, lakes, and even rivers. Irrigation canals were also part of the land gift, with their maintenance being the responsibility of those using them.

Terracing was practiced for centuries on irrigated fields to grow corn, potatoes, and other vegetables.

Crops

In these irrigated fields, the Incas and their subjects raised a number of crops. The most important food crop was maize, or corn, since it was easily dried and stored for long periods of time. Prepared as it still is in western South America, corn was boiled to a soft paste or roasted to a hard kernel. Sometimes it was turned into popcorn or made into corn beer, which were favorites all over the empire. Corn beer, known as *chicha*, was also used in religious ceremonies.

Potatoes were almost as important a food as corn. They were stored for long periods after alternately freezing and drying them. Additionally, imperial farmers grew sweet potatoes, tomatoes, squash, beans, and chili peppers.

Cotton was the most valuable of the nonfood crops, but gourds, which when dried and hollowed out supplied vessels to carry and store water, were also prized. Additionally, farmers grew coca, which was mixed with lime and chewed as a protection from fatigue and cold. The emperor himself normally had a bag of coca hanging from his waist.

A portion of the crops from the emperor's fields went to feed the imperial household, but much of the harvest was placed in imperial storehouses. This stored food made up a large part of the empire's wealth and was used as gifts or as emergency rations in times of famine.

The produce from the temple lands went to feed priests, priestesses, and other temple attendants. Some of it was used in religious rites.

Barter

Although householders did not own their own land, they did own whatever crops were raised on it. Commoner households were allowed to trade any excess food they produced for other types of food, clothing, tools, or cookware. Without money, all trade was barter, which involved bargaining, since no set value for anything existed. Thus, for instance, trading corn for a ceramic cooking pot required the respective owners to bargain until they agreed on how much corn a pot was worth.

Nevertheless, Incan communities had no central place for the trading of food and goods. After extensive excavations of the Incan city of Huánuco Pampa, archaeologists Craig Morris and Donald E. Thompson found no evidence of market activity. Moreover, they report that their "coverage of the city was sufficiently complete to suggest that no major spaces were given over to market style exchange. Products of the fields . . . were exchanged instead among people related by kinship or political ties, and . . . these exchanges do not appear to have involved gathering at some common marketplace."[31]

Besides local trade, some trade between regions of the empire existed. However, this trade was the monopoly of the emperor.

Mining and Herding

In addition to agricultural fields, land that contained mines was valued. Gold, silver, and copper were much prized for making tools and jewelry. In general, the emperor did not share mining real estate with others. Still, Spanish accounts indicate that some mines northeast of Lake Titicaca were set aside for use by the local population.

Like land, llamas and alpacas were precious. They were treasured for their wool and meat and for the llama's worth as a pack animal. Although the emperor kept possession of the majority of the herds, he allowed the temples to keep animals for ritual sacrifice. Further, individual households were permitted to have up to ten animals. All the livestock of an ayllu was normally herded together, with each family notching the ears or branding the flanks to mark its particular llamas or alpacas.

Labor Taxes

In the Incan Empire, a society without machines, human labor was so important in

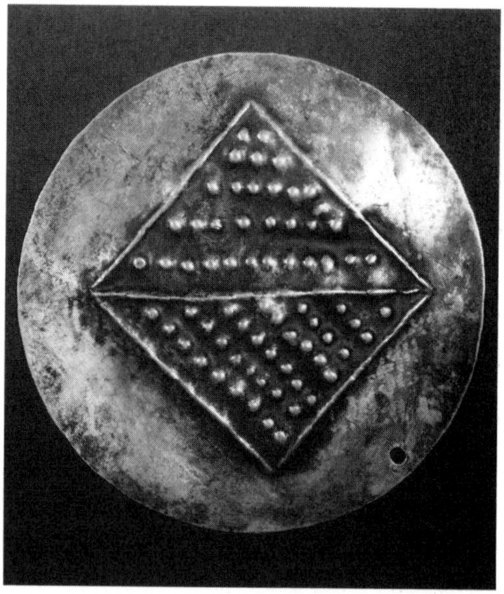

Prized precious metals were made into tools and jewelry, such as this ornamental silver disc.

INCAN KNOWLEDGE

Incan education for aristocratic boys consisted in part of mathematics, geography, and music. Garcilaso de la Vega, the seventeenth-century part-Incan chronicler, explains in his *Royal Commentaries of the Incas and General History of Peru* what the Incas understood about these subjects.

> [The Incas] knew a great deal of geometry because this was necessary for measuring their lands, and adjusting the boundaries and dividing them. But this was physical knowledge, obtained with strings and stones used for counting and dividing, and nothing to do with heights [measured] in degrees. . . .
>
> In geography they were able to depict, and each tribe could model and draw its towns and provinces as they had seen them. They did not trouble about other provinces. Their skill in this was extreme. I saw the model of Cuzco and part of the surrounding area in clay, pebbles, and sticks. It was done to scale with the [city] squares, large and small; the streets, broad and narrow; the districts and houses, even the most obscure; and the three streams that flow through the city, marvelously executed. The countryside with high hills and low, flats and ravines, rivers and streams with their twists and turns were all wonderfully rendered, and the best cosmographer [geographer] in the world could not have done it better. . . .
>
> They knew a great deal of arithmetic. . . .
>
> In music they understood certain modes, which . . . [they] played on . . . reed pipes. Four or five reeds were bound side by side, each a little higher than the last, like organ pipes. . . . One gave the low notes, another higher, and the other higher still, like the four natural voices: treble, tenor, contralto, and bass.

getting work done that people paid labor taxes. The empire had two such taxes: the *mit'a* and an agricultural tax. To pay the *mit'a*, each household sent one of its male members to work for the imperial government. The *mit'a* came due every year, and its period of service varied from a few days to a few months.

Mit'a workers built the cities, the roads, and the agricultural terraces. They worked in the mines and carried crops from the fields to the storehouses. They served in the homes of the nobles, and they soldiered in the army.

To pay the agricultural tax, householders had to help plant, tend, and harvest the crops that belonged to the emperor and the temples. The commoners also looked after the imperial and temple herds.

Women were exempt from the *mit'a*. However, they, as well as their children, worked in the fields of the emperor and the temples. Additionally, once a year, the women of each household had to make at least one woven garment, which went into the empire's warehouses. Stored clothing was distributed as gifts to aristocrats and to soldiers serving in the army. It also went to people who had lost all their possessions in house fires, earthquakes, and floods.

Emperor and Prefects

The exact process of imperial decision making is not known. What projects would be undertaken? How many *mit'a* workers would be needed for how long? Neither archaeologists nor historians have provided answers. Even the size of the imperial government is unknown.

Nonetheless, the Spanish chronicles make it clear that general policy was made by the emperor in consultation with senior advisers. These advisers were prefects, or *apos*. Headquartered in Cuzco and relatives of the Sapa Inca, they were well-seasoned, experienced government officials.

Each *apo* was also in charge of one of the four major divisions, or quarters, of the empire. All of these divisions began at Cuzco and radiated out, making the empire look like a pie sliced into quarters. The sections were not of equal size. To the north was Chinchaysuyu and to the south, Collasuyu, the two largest divisions. The considerably smaller segments were east and west—Antisuyu and Cuntisuyu, respectively. The job of each prefect was to see that the emperor's orders were carried out in his division.

Provincial Governors

The four quarters of the empire were further divided into some eighty provinces. Each province roughly equaled one conquered realm. Some of the larger conquests such as Chimú occupied more than one province, while some of the smaller were lumped together, making provinces of about the same size.

In charge of each province was a provincial governor, known as the *tocricoc apo*. Like the *apos*, *tocricoc apos* were Incan nobles, often members of the royal family. Provincial governors had two major responsibilities. They enforced imperial law, and they looked after the interests of the people of their province.

Provincial Capitals

Each province had an administrative center, a capital city built to house the governor, his staff, and other imperial officers. It was here that the barracks for *mit'a* workers were located. In these centers, artisans manufactured sturdy, functional pottery for the commoners. These centers also served as gathering places for major religious ceremonies. According to Morris and von Hagen, excavations of these sites reveal that

> their architecture, and usually their pottery and other portable artifacts, immediately identify the centers as . . . [different from] the local system of towns and villages. They counted members of the ruling elite from Cuzco among their population. . . . Most of the people who used . . . [their] facilities . . . came for relatively short periods to pay their labor tax while living as guests of the Inka [*sic*], whose storehouses provided for them during their stay.[32]

IMPERIAL STOREHOUSES

The Inca Empire had thousands of storehouses filled with food and goods, which represented much of the realm's wealth. Archaeologists Craig Morris and Donald E. Thompson studied the remains of these structures at the provincial Incan city of Huánuco Pampa. Their findings are in *Huánuco Pampa: An Inca City and Its Hinterlands*.

> Long lines of storehouses overlook Huánuco Pampa from a hill to the south. Approaching the city on the Inca road from Quito to Cajamarca . . . one can see the warehouses from more than 30 km [18 miles] before actually reaching the city, announcing the wealth of the [Sapa] Inca and the security of his installation. . . .
>
> The state warehouses of the Inca, at least in the Peruvian central highlands, have three . . . characteristics. Instead of regular doors with a threshold at ground surface, they have one or more window-like openings. They are normally placed in rows on a hillside above any residential structures that may be associated with them. And, finally, in the excavated sample that had . . . pottery [in it], that pottery was overwhelmingly large, narrow-neck jars. . . .
>
> The warehouses take two forms, rectangular and circular. The windows of the circular face uphill. The rectangular [storehouses] . . . of the top row and the third row from the top have a single room. Those of the second and fourth rows from the top are usually divided into two rooms. . . . Only two structures have more than two rooms. . . .
>
> The storage of maize . . . seems to be limited to circular structures. . . . Not all circular structures were reserved for maize. While only root crops [potatoes] were identified in rectangular [warehouses] . . . , the sample is so small that we cannot conclude that rectangular storehouses were devoted . . . to tubers.

These are ruins of Incan storehouses, which were once filled with food and goods for wartime or famine.

IMPERIAL LAW

In the Inca Empire, those guilty of crimes often faced torture and death. Jesuit Bernabe Cobo, in his *History of the Inca Empire*, written in 1653, provides a summary of Incan law, which favored the nobility over the commoners and men over women.

> He that killed another to rob him received the death penalty, and before it was executed, the guilty person was tortured. . . .
>
> If someone was killed in a quarrel, first it was determined who caused it; if the dead man did, the killer was given a light punishment . . . ; if the one who caused the fight was the slayer, he received the death penalty, or at the very best, he was exiled . . . [to] serve for his whole life in the Inca's . . . coca fields. . . .
>
> The husband that killed his wife for adultery was set free without punishment, but if he killed her due to anger . . . , he received the death penalty if he was an ordinary man, but if he was an important gentleman [aristocrat] . . . , he did not die, but he was given another punishment.
>
> The woman that killed her husband received the death penalty. . . . She was hung up by the feet in some public place, and she was left like that until she died. . . .
>
> In certain cases marriage was prohibited, and fornication [sexual relations] in the cases in which marriage was prohibited was punishable with the death penalty, if the guilty party was not a noble, because a noble got only a public reprimand. . . .
>
> He that robbed without reason, besides paying for the stolen item if he had the resources, was exiled. . . .
>
> He that stole things to eat from necessity was reprimanded and given no other punishment.

Each capital had some five hundred storehouses, built in rows along nearby hillsides. This height protected the contents from getting wet, but it also made a grand display to the local people of the wealth and power of the Incas. The storehouses were spaced sufficiently far apart to keep fire from spreading easily from one to another. Found in the storehouses were food, clothes, weapons and other military equipment, and tools. The Incan capital of Cuzco also had a large number of warehouses, as did some of the other provincial cities.

The *Curacas*

A single province was home to twenty thousand households. The imperial government split these families into two sections of ten thousand apiece. Each section was further subdivided into two clusters of five thousand households. The division continued through groups of one thousand households, five hundred, and finally one hundred.

Administration of these different-sized household units was in the hands of the *curacas*, with two senior officials overseeing the ten-thousand-household sections. The *curacas* were the ones who actually saw to it that the correct number of people showed up for *mit'a* labor or for working the imperial and temple lands. They also had to supervise the collection and transportation of harvested crops and other goods to storage facilities.

Enforcing the Law

The provincial governor rewarded *curacas* who did their jobs well with luxuries. Senior *curacas* could expect gifts of servants, secondary wives, and even land and livestock from the emperor himself. However, a *curaca* who did a poor job was punished by the provincial governor. If the *curaca* was judged lazy or incompetent, he was publicly reprimanded and dismissed. If he was dishonest or cruel, he was executed.

Major officials at all levels of the Incan government acted as judges, depending on the nature of the case. Minor disputes, such as fights between husbands and wives or arguments between neighbors, were brought before the local *curaca*, who listened to the complaints of the parties involved and then rendered a judgment.

More weighty matters, such as theft, rape, and murder, were judged by the provincial governor, who alone in a province had the power to grant life or death. The accused was brought to the provincial capital, although by whom is not known, and kept in jail until the trial. On the day of the trial, both accused and accuser presented their cases to the provincial governor. Witnesses might also be heard. After the testimony, the governor decided then and there whether the accused was innocent or guilty. If declared innocent, the accused was freed.

If the verdict was guilty, punishment followed quickly, often as soon as the trial was over. Punishment was often harsh: Torture and execution were common sentences for everything from adultery to burning down government buildings. Some crimes, such as treason and practicing black magic, called for the entire family of the person convicted to be clubbed or stoned to death.

Language

The Incan government could function only if its many people and parts could talk with one another. That demanded a single language, which was Quechua. Thus, the Incas required *curacas* to master Quechua and ordered that commoners teach their children the language.

However, the empire did not insist on people giving up their native speech. And for a time, many of the realm's inhabitants were bilingual. However, the constant use of Quechua generally eclipsed a subject people's original language. Later the Spanish would find Quechua as worthwhile as the Incas and would continue its use. To this day, Andeans speak among themselves almost exclusively in Quechua.

Keeping Local Ways

The Incas allowed their subjects to keep more than their original languages. Indeed, the emperor and imperial officials found it to their advantage to leave local customs and religions alone as much as possible. The Incas commanded, of course, that each conquered people take its place in Incan society and that its members participate in Incan state religious ceremonies. Otherwise, the folk were allowed to keep their own dress, their own gods, their own coming-of-age rites, and so on.

Accordingly, any concessions that did not undercut Incan authority nor lessen the efficiency of the workforce were granted to imperial subjects. This policy of tolerance reduced resentment toward Incan rule and toward the payment of the labor taxes.

Resettlement

The tolerance policy, however, did not interfere with the Incas' need for control. As historian Rebecca Stone-Miller writes, they "captured foreign leaders, artisans, and religious icons [ancestral mummies and other sacred relics] . . . and held them hostage in Cuzco."[33] Such actions were designed to guarantee obedience to the empire, whose needs came before all else.

Sometimes those needs demanded great sacrifices from commoners. For example, if a province lacked enough people to work all its productive land or to meet its *mit'a* obligations, imperial officials forced households from more densely populated provinces to leave their homes and migrate to the place that needed workers. If the local population increased sufficiently, the transported workers eventually returned home. Otherwise, their move was permanent.

The Incas also used resettlement as a way of dealing with rebellion. Troublemaking groups would find themselves far from their homes, living in unknown territory, and generally surrounded by loyal Incan subjects. Still other loyal households were then ordered to move to the rebels' original homeland.

Tax Exemptions

Imperial policy also allowed for tax exemptions, and a number of classes and professions were excused from paying the labor taxes. The entire imperial aristocracy, including the *curacas*, as a class paid no taxes. Indeed, few of them, men or women, did much manual work. Servants attended to their fields and their houses.

There were also commoners who were exempted from the *mit'a*. One such group was the *yanaconas*. Many of the servants of the nobility were fulfilling their *mit'a* duty, particularly those who worked for the *curacas*. They thus rotated in and out of aristocratic households.

The *yanaconas*, on the other hand, formed a corps of permanent servants. Their positions were hereditary, with children following parents into service. Their original members were rebels who had been sentenced to lifetime work in the houses and fields of the upper class. Although many *yanaconas* worked in lowly positions, some showed such talent for management that they were given government posts.

A second class of tax-exempt commoners possessed such valuable, specialized skills that they worked only at a single profession, which was hereditary. Among these professionals were the artisans who created gold and silver jewelry work, fine textiles, and elegant ceramics.

Reading the Knots

Other professionals excused from taxes were the *quipucamayocs*, the imperial accountants. The Incas may have lacked writing, but they had an accounting system. Imper-

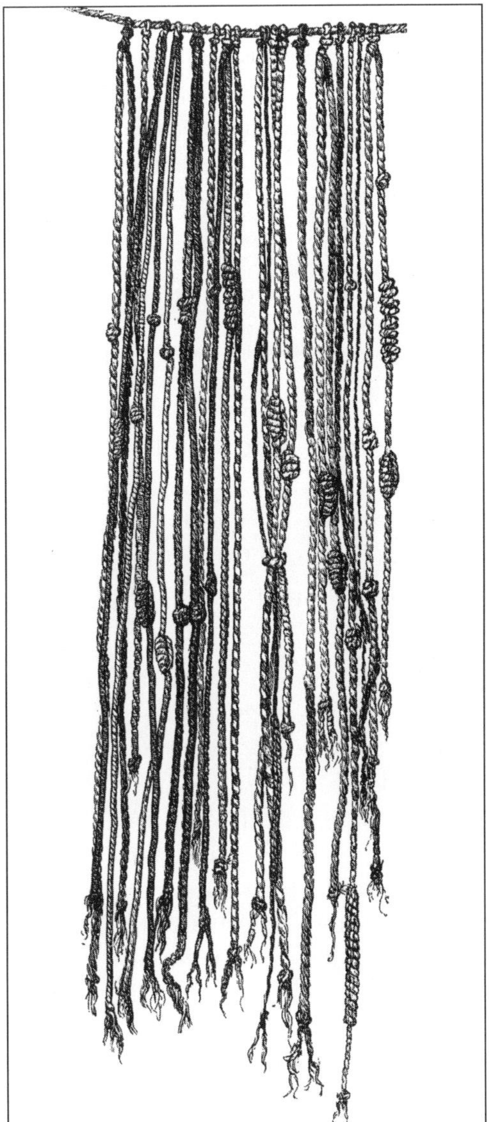

The quipa—a counting device with knotted wool strings—made it possible for the empire to keep detailed records.

ial accounts told officials, for instance, how many households were in a particular area or how much corn was harvested and stored or how large the llama herds were.

The Incas recorded these accounts on the quipu, a collection of knotted wool strings. Each quipu had a long main cord from which dangled different colored strings. Some surviving quipus have hundreds of threads attached to the central cord.

Each string had a series of knots of different sizes. The size and position of the knots represented numbers. Those at the bottom—that is, farthest from the main cord—were one through nine. Knots in a string's middle were ten through ninety-nine, and those at the top, one hundred and above. Additionally, scholars believe that the point from which a string hung from the main cord identified the item being tallied—corn perhaps, or clothing or even people.

A second type of quipu had geometric designs and other symbols tied to the strings. It was used to help people remember Incan history, songs, and poems. The symbols represented ideas or classes of events that made it easier to recall the full version of stories passed along orally.

The Accountants

The task of the *quipucamayocs* was to read the quipus. Each *quipucamayoc* was a specialist. Some read only crop accounts, others *mit'a* records, and still others military and religious accounts.

These quipu readers were scattered throughout the empire, living in cities, towns, and villages. Although a *quipucamayoc* worked closely with local *curacas*, he was answerable only to the provincial governor. As with other commoners exempt from the general labor tax, *quipucamayocs* occupieda hereditary position, with each accountant teaching his son the knot code.

Recovering the Code

Over the centuries, the knot code was lost, but in 1912, Leland L. Locke of the New York Museum of Natural History worked out the numerical reading of the quipu. According to archaeologist Laura Laurencich Minelli, "Locke noted that there were different ranges [positions] of knots . . . ; There were long knots . . . with a maximum of 9 turns. . . . Locke deduced that the long knots indicated numbers 2 to 9 [through the number of turns in a knot]. . . . String without knots . . . [were] zero."[34]

Locke was immediately able to read one four-string sequence as seventeen. The first string was zero; the second, ten; the third, six; and the final, one. The remainder of the code—what people or goods were being counted—continues to be a mystery.

COMPOUND OF THE CHOSEN WOMEN

Archaeologists Craig Morris and Donald E. Thompson spent years excavating the ruins of the provincial Incan city of Huánuco Pampa. In their *Huánuco Pampa: An Inca City and Its Hinterlands*, they describe the quarters of the Chosen Women of the city.

> [A] compound . . . is located at the edge of the main plaza. . . . It consists of fifty buildings surrounded by a wall and represents some of the most vigorously planned architecture in the city. . . . Several bone-weaving implements and dozens of ceramic spindle whorls [also for weaving] indicate spinning and weaving as a major activity. Hundreds, if not thousands, of large ceramic jars of a kind believed to have been used for making *chichi*, the native maize beer, indicate that brewing was another major activity. Since the manufacture of cloth and beer for the state is attributed in the [Spanish] written sources to . . . [the] *aklla* [Chosen Women], it is . . . reasonable . . . that a group of these women occupied this compound. . . . Access to the compound is tightly controlled. The only entrance is a narrow door in the southern side of the . . . [compound] wall. . . . One [then] passes through a small courtyard onto which opens a single building . . . [with a] door . . . in its end. . . . It is then necessary to go through a tiny square building to reach an open courtyard that appears to have been the . . . public area of the compound. The apparent emphasis on control and security is in keeping with . . . seclusion for the 'chosen women.' The regular rows of rectangular buildings in the northern part of the compound constitute [make up] a . . . barracks-like architecture, suggesting a non-family occupying unit. The great density of refuse [trash] in the compound suggests permanent occupation.

The Chosen Women

One of the most important groups of full-time workers in the Inca Empire was the Chosen Women, or *acllas*. These women came from all social classes: the Cuzco nobility, the families of *curacas*, and the commoners. They were selected by an imperial official, who sought out pretty and good-natured nine- and ten-year-old girls.

The girls then went to school either at Cuzco or the nearest provincial administrative center, where, as anthropologist George Bankes writes, they were "taught . . . religion and how to dye, spin and weave cotton and wool to a high standard. Their training also included cooking and making fine chicha."[35]

At thirteen or fourteen, the trained *acllas* were presented to the emperor. The Sapa Inca chose a few of the young women to be his secondary wives, while others were given as gifts to favored nobles.

Aclla Service

Of the remaining Chosen Women, some went to serve in the temples, while others returned to their schools to teach new *acllas*. Still others spent their lives making the many elaborate garments that the emperor and the Incan aristocracy wore. Many took up posts cooking and making *chicha* for the *mit'a* work gangs.

Archaeologists have found evidence for *aclla* activity at Huánuco Pampa. Morris and von Hagen report that "excavations at a place where they [Chosen Women] lived and worked . . . uncovered hundreds of spinning and weaving implements [tools] and large numbers of broken jars once used in brewing."[36]

Even more than most people in the empire, the Chosen Women were tightly controlled. Except for those who became secondary wives, they were forbidden to marry or have lovers. They had to perform whatever tasks were set before them.

Despite this lack of freedom, the *acllas* were among the most respected members of the empire. Their roles in cloth production and as *mit'a* support staff made significant contributions to the Incan economy. Their service to the Incan temples also enhanced their reputation, for the state religion was extremely important to the Incas and to the empire.

Chapter Five

Gods and Priests

The Inca Empire was united by more than administrative control. It depended also on religion to tie its people together. The Incas imposed their religion on conquered people, but as an overlay, not as a substitute, for local gods and beliefs. Indeed, as Baudin observes, "the Incas showed respect for the beliefs of the nations they subdued."[37] Since Incan religion and other Andean faiths had the same cultural roots and thus many shared beliefs, tolerating other practices was not difficult for the Incas.

However, the empire needed its subjects to be members of the state religion, which was an important political tool. Through ritual and instruction, Incan priests promoted the idea that the Incas had the goodwill and protection of the gods, that their imperial expansion was a divine mission.

In no way does this practical use of religion mean that the Incas lacked conviction or religious fervor. Sincerity of belief made their claims of being on a divine mission stronger and more convincing.

The Creator

The Incan religion had many gods. Chief among these deities was Viracocha, hailed as the creator of the world and all the other gods. It was said that Viracocha made humanity in his own image and then brought light into the world when, after crafting them, he pulled the Sun and the Moon from an island in Lake Titicaca.

Spanish descriptions of Viracocha's statues had the god posed with right arm raised, the fist clenched, except for thumb and forefinger. In the temple at Cuzco, his statue was a solid-gold, four-foot-high figure of a young boy. The eighth emperor, Viracocha Inca, was named after this creator god.

The Sun

Below Viracocha were three major gods: Inti, the Sun God; Illapa, the Thunder God; and Mama-Quilla, the Moon God. These were the sky gods, and their importance rested in their control of light and rain, crucial to farming.

Inti the Sun was the god of agriculture and was the most powerful of the three. In addition to crops, the Sun God also produced gold, and thus, according to Constance Classen, gold "represented timeless, ideal structure. As such it was used for the creation of sacred models [statues]."[38] Inti himself was shown as a gold disk with rays projecting from the rim and a human face in the center.

The Sun was the patron of the Incas because he was supposedly the ancestor of the Sapa Inca, who called himself the Son of the Sun. By tradition, Pachacuti Inca Yupanqui had announced this link between Incan royalty and divinity after Inti came to him in a dream. As Fagan notes, "In time, the people came to believe they were under Inti's protection, and that their leaders were descended from this deity."[39]

The divine nature of the Sapa Inca, and by extension the empire, was crucial support for the Incas' belief that they had the right to conquer and rule. The emperor's claim that he was part god made it easy for imperial officials to argue that the empire's economic and social policies were god-inspired and god-protected. Consequently, the empire literally had a god-given right to the labor of their subjects.

Sky and Earth

Illapa controlled the weather and the rain and was portrayed as a man in glowing clothes standing in the sky. In one hand was a club and in the other, a sling. Mama-Quilla, the third sky god, was always shown as a woman and was Inti's wife, although she had no specific powers. Legend has it that when Viracocha created the Moon, she was as bright as the Sun. A jealous Inti threw ashes on her face, dimming her light.

A whole host of other gods occupied positions beneath the sky gods. Pacha-Mama, another female deity, was the Earth God, who made the fields fertile and who shook the ground with earthquakes. Mama-Cocha, the female Sea God, was the source of all water—ocean, rivers, lakes, springs, and even irrigation water. Other gods oversaw the llama and alpaca herds and plants and seeds, among many other tasks. Each was identified with a specific star or constellation.

Incas present gifts to Inti, the Sun God. Food, gold, and other possesions were offered in exchange for the help and protection of a deity.

Spirit World

The Incas also believed that the world contained spirits. These spirits were often associated with places and objects, called *huacas*. Scholars are unsure whether *huacas* were spirits or merely the dwelling places of supernatural beings.

Among the *huacas* were temples, tombs, hills, bridges, fountains, springs, lakes, and rivers. The caves south of Cuzco from which Manco Capac and the Incas reportedly emerged were holy sites. Amulets, or charms, were portable *huacas* that were worn as necklaces or bracelets.

Sacred Stones

The most common *huacas* were rocks. Piles of stones generally marked all *huacas*. Passersby would add a pebble or rock to a pile.

Scholars Michael Coe, Dean Snow, and Elizabeth Benson write:

> All pre-Columbian people [in the Western Hemisphere] seem to have had sacred or special stones, but the Inca went further with this practice than any other people. . . . Manco Capac, the first Inca ruler, . . . is said to have marked off the land [of the Incas] by throwing four . . . stones toward the four corners of the earth. It was believed that Manco Capac eventually . . . turned to stone and, as such, was carried into battle by later Inca warriors. . . . All around Cuzco sacred stones fan out from the city, some plain and weathered, some natural rocks carved with step[s] . . . , serpentine [snake-like] forms and other designs.[40]

In addition to Manco Capac, two of his brothers turned to stone. One of these alleged hardened bodies sat atop a hill near Cuzco and was one of the most sacred spots in the empire.

Other sacred rocks were the stones that legend said had aided in the defense of Cuzco against the Chanca. Even some quarries were sometimes holy sites.

Afterlife

Included among the *huacas* were the mummified bodies of the dead, particularly of the former emperors. The Incas believed that the souls of the dead looked after their descendants. To repay ancestors for this watchfulness, Incas seated the bodies at feasts, where shares of food and beer were set out before the mummies.

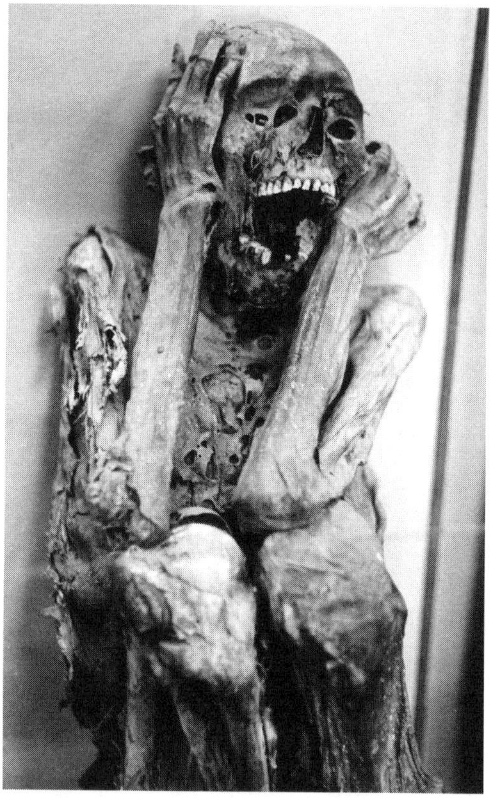

Mummies like this one were brought out at feasts where Incas honored their ancestors.

CORICANCHA, CUZCO'S TEMPLE OF THE SUN

In *The Incas*, sixteenth-century chronicler Pedro de Cieza de León gives a detailed description of Coricancha, the main temple at Cuzco. This temple was not a building but a compound that contained several buildings within its walls.

> [The temple] had many gates, and the gateways finely carved; halfway up the wall ran a stripe of gold. . . . The gateway and doors were covered with this metal. Inside there were four buildings, . . . and the walls [of each] inside and out were covered with gold. . . . There were two benches . . . , which the rising sun fell upon. . . . These benches were for the Lord-Incas [emperors], and if anyone else sat there, he was sentenced to death.
>
> There were guards at the doors of these houses whose duty it was to watch over the virgins [Chosen Women], . . . the most beautiful . . . that could be found. They remained in the temples until they were old. . . .
>
> Around this temple there were many small dwellings of Indians who were assigned to its service, and there was a fence inside which they put the white lambs [llamas], children and men to be sacrificed. . . .
>
> The high priest . . . dwelt in the temple. . . . Within the temple there were more than thirty bins [made] of silver in which they stored the corn, and the contributions of many provinces were assigned to this temple. . . .
>
> I make no mention of the silverwork, beads, golden feathers, and other things which if I were to describe them, would not be believed.

The Incan religion had a heaven and a hell. An individual who led a good life went to live with the Sun, while one who was bad ended up living beneath the earth. All Incan nobility, no matter how they behaved, automatically ended up in heaven, while commoners had to earn the right, probably in part by being good, obedient subjects of the emperor. Afterlife with the Sun was the same as life on earth, except there was always enough to eat and drink. Under the earth, it was cold, and hunger was the norm.

The Temples

Every major Incan city had a temple. The Spanish would later call all these structures Sun Temples. In reality, each of these buildings housed all the gods, not just Inti. However, only Viracocha, Inti, and Illapa were usually represented by statues or paintings.

The Incas did not worship inside their temples, but rather outside of them, generally in a city's plaza or town square. One exception may have been the temple near the modern Peruvian city of San Pedro Cacha. Its ruins reveal a large open interior, which may have been used for ceremonies.

Most temples were storehouses for priestly garments and holy artifacts. They were also filled with gold and silver statues and beautiful textiles, testifying to the Incas' wealth and prestige. At Coricancha, the great temple of Cuzco, considered the center of both the empire and the world, Inti was represented by a huge disk of gold embedded with gems. Sitting on thrones of gold and facing this disk were life-sized carved images of the former emperors.

In another part of Coricancha was an artificial garden filled with sculpted corn plants. The Spanish would later be struck by the detail work that showed stalks and kernels. They were even more impressed that the plants and even the garden soil from which the corn rose were solid gold. Next to this garden was a set of llamas and their young, surrounded by shepherds, all crafted from gold.

The royal mummies may also have been stashed in Coricancha, or they may have been housed in the palaces of their respective ayllus. The Spanish chronicles are not clear on this matter.

Priesthood

The temples were also the living quarters of the priests and priestesses. Both priests and priestesses were members of the Incan nobility. The men conducted services to the male gods and the women to the female. Each deity had its own set of clergy, with those serving Inti ranked highest.

Priests were specialists. Some heard confession, some predicted the future, and some managed the fields that fed and clothed the clergy. Some inherited their positions, while others became priests because they were blind or deaf or even because they were struck by lightning—all signs that they had been touched by the gods. All began their training as young boys.

Nothing is known about the exact duties of priestesses beyond their serving the female gods. How they were selected and trained is also unknown.

The High Priest

The high priest, who was also the head priest of Inti, was a close relative of the Sapa Inca. In theory, the emperor was the head of the religion, as he was the head of state. However, his religious duties were confined to officiating at only very important ceremonies. Day-to-day administration was left to the high priest.

A high priest, like the one depicted here, performed the day-to-day rituals of the empire.

HARVEST CELEBRATION

The Incas had many religious festivals during the year. In June, they celebrated the corn harvest, as the soldier Pedro de Cieza de León describes in *The Incas*, written in 1553.

> To celebrate this feast with greater devotion . . . , it is said that they fasted for ten to twelve days, refraining from eating much and sleeping with their women. . . . When this had been done, they . . . [had] large numbers of . . . llamas, pigeons, guinea pigs, and other birds and animals which were killed as sacrifice. . . . They anointed [covered] the statues and figures of their gods . . . with the blood, and the doors of the temples . . . , where they hung the entrails [intestines]; and after a time the soothsayers and oracles . . . [examined them] for signs. . . .
>
> When the sacrifice had been made, the high priest and the other priests . . . ordered the mamaconas [Chosen Women] to come forth richly attired and with a great quantity of . . . chicha . . . , serving it in goblets of gold from . . . tubs of silver. . . .
>
> In the middle of the plaza they had erected . . . a great . . . [throne], covered with cloth of feathers thick with beads of gold, and great blankets of their finest wool, embroidered in gold and jewels. At the top of this throne, they placed the figure of . . . Viracocha, large and richly adorned. . . . And the Inca [emperor] with the nobles and the common people . . . , removing their sandals, . . . bending their backs and puffing out their cheeks, . . . blew their breath toward him. . . .
>
> Below this throne there was the image of the sun . . . and that of the moon. . . . The statues of the dead Incas were brought out. . . . Many people . . . laid before them . . . little idols of gold, and llamas of gold, and figures of women, all small, and many other jewels.

Elected by the aristocracy for life, the high priest was one of the most powerful people in the Inca Empire. Kendall writes that he "was so revered that he competed in authority with the Sapa Inca. He had power over all . . . temples, to which he appointed priests."[41]

Virgins of the Sun

Besides the clergy, the temples were served by attendants. The Virgins of the Sun were chief among these servants. They were the Chosen Women, the *acllas*, assigned to religious duty. Their responsibilities included making *chicha*, which was used frequently in ceremonies; cooking food that was given in sacrifice to the gods; and weaving clothes for the priests as well as for gifts to the gods.

The virginity of these women was jealously guarded, as it was for all *acllas* except those who had become secondary wives. As with Incan justice in general, punishment was harsh for *acllas* who took lovers; both man and woman were hung up by the hair to die.

Ritual Offerings

Ceremony and the ritual that accompanied it were at the heart of Incan religion. Theology took a back seat, as Bankes observes:

> Inca religion was mainly concerned with . . . ritual rather than mysticism and spirituality. Divination [forecasting the future] was regarded as important . . . [before taking] any action. . . . It was particularly important for the individual to ensure that the supernatural forces of the environment were kept in a benevolent mood, otherwise physical or economic misfortune might befall him.[42]

Sacrifice, offering something of value to a god, was an important part of almost every Incan ceremony. Just as goods were exchanged for service around the empire, they were offered in religious rites as payment for supernatural aid.

Sometimes the sacrifice was food and coca, which would be burned, and *chicha*, which was poured on the ground. Fancy textiles, seashells, gold, and silver were also offered.

Animal Sacrifice

Llamas were a favorite offering. Each major god had its particular color animal. Thus, Viracocha received a brown llama; Inti, a white; and Illapa, a mixed-color animal. After the priest cut the sacrificial llama's throat, he smeared its blood over the image of the god.

Llamas were also used in prophesying the future. After killing the animal, a priest removed a lung and studied the patterns on its surface.

When an imperial heir was named, a priestly examination of a llama's intestines was undertaken. If the reading was favorable, the candidate was judged suitable to be emperor. If the signs were not favorable, he was supposedly rejected and a new heir named. Like many aspects of Incan life, to what extent this ceremony influenced imperial succession is not known.

Human Sacrifice

Like the Moche and other Andean people, the Incas practiced human sacrifice, the most valuable of all offerings. Such sacrifice was rare because it was reserved for very important events, such as the coronation or death of an emperor. Ceremonies in response to natural disasters and war also called for human sacrifice.

Most of the sacrificial victims were children between the ages of ten and fifteen because children were purer of spirit than adults. These children were always non-Incans. Boys were collected from commoner households as another form of taxation. Girls came from the most beautiful of the Sun Virgins.

According to the eminent archaeologist John Howland Rowe, this practice "may have had some unifying effect. . . . Selected boys and girls were . . . distributed for sacrifice to the major shrines [temples] of the realm."[43] Some even made months-long pilgrimages from province to province, where they were treated with great reverence. Being a sacrifice was considered a great honor among the Incas and the other Andean people, including the victims and their families. The sacrificed child was being sent to live with the gods—indeed, to become a minor deity.

Ice Mummies

Most of the children were sacrificed during ceremonies held in or near cities. A few, however, took place atop some of the highest and, to the Incans, holiest of mountains, such as Pichu Pichu and the volcano Nevado Ampato, both in Peru. Priests took the children up to the summits of these peaks, where the victims were killed and buried.

Because children were purer of spirit than adults, they were used more often in human sacrifices. Shown is the mummified remains of a sacrificed Incan girl.

Both Pichu Pichu and Ampato are four miles high. At that altitude, the air is thin and very dry, with temperatures that never rise much above freezing even in the summer. These cold, dry conditions mummified the bodies.

In the 1990s, anthropologist Johan Reinhard of the National Geographic Society uncovered half a dozen of these ice mummies on Pichu Pichu and Ampato, as well as on a mountain in Argentina. The condition of the bodies varied from excellent to poor. Two bodies had mostly decayed, despite the altitude, and one had been badly burned by a lightning strike.

Secrets of the Dead

All of the corpses, however, revealed many aspects of the Incan sacrificial rite. At least one of the children had eaten before being killed. This discovery confirmed Spanish accounts of victims feasting before sacrifice so that they would not go to the gods hungry.

Often the children were unconscious by the feast's end from having drunk goodly amounts of *chicha* and were often killed before they could wake up. Reinhard is convinced that the serene faces of the Argentinean children show that they were unconscious and unaware of approaching death.

A CT scan of the head of a young girl found on Ampato showed that she had been killed with a blow struck just above her right eye. Others were probably smothered or strangled. All these forms of execution are mentioned in Spanish accounts, as are cutting victims' throats, burying them alive, and tearing their still-beating hearts from their chests.

Treasures of the Dead

Reinhard's mummies were richly dressed and were buried with expensive goods. One

INCAN PRAYERS

According to Louis Baudin in his *Daily Life in Peru Under the Last Incas*, the following were two popular Incan prayers. The first was probably addressed to Viracocha, the chief Incan god, while the second was aimed at Inti, the Sun God, from whom the emperor claimed descent.

> O Creator! thou who art at the ends of the earth, thou who givest life and soul to men, and sayest to each man, 'Be thou such a kind of man,' and to each woman, 'Be thou such a kind of woman,' thou who, speaking thus, didst create and fashion them and didst give them life. Protect these men whom thou hast made, that they may live safe and sound, sheltered from danger, and in peace. Where art thou? In the highest heaven or in the depth of the thunder and the storm clouds? Hear thou, answer me, be kindly disposed towards me. Give us life eternal, hold us in thy hand, and receive this offering wherever thou mayst be, O Creator!"
>
> "O Creator! May the subjects of the Inca [emperor], the peoples in subjugation to him, and his servants, rest in safety and peace in the reign of thy son, the Inca, whom thou has given us as king. Whilst his reign lasts, may thy people multiply and be kept safe, may it be for them an age of prosperity, may everything increase, fields, men, and beasts, and guide always with thy hand the monarch to whom thou has given birth, O Creator!

young girl had on an elaborate feathered headdress and was covered by a man's shirt, one of fancy design normally reserved for the aristocracy. A boy had an extra set of sandals and was wearing a too-large shirt, into which he was apparently expected to grow while living with the gods.

With the bodies were placed gold and silver figurines of llamas and people. Silver shawl pins and a seashell necklace were found with one of the girls. Most of the clothing and artifacts excavated by Reinhard were definitely Incan in design, even those discovered on the Argentinean mountain a thousand miles from Cuzco.

Ceremony

The ceremonies surrounding the sacrifices on Pichu Pichu and Ampato were seen by very few, although probably large, well-attended rituals were conducted prior to the ascent of the mountains. Attendance at ceremonies probably varied according to the importance of the event. Of the regular ceremonies, those held in May, June, and December were the most important. In May, the Incas celebrated the corn harvest and in December the beginning of the rainy season. The festival in June was dedicated to Inti, and only Incas of royal blood were permitted to participate.

Additionally, the Incas had small daily ceremonies, most notably offerings of wood, cloth, and food to the Sun. They also had special ceremonies to ask the god's assistance with some threat, such as drought.

The Incas prepared for major ceremonies by bathing and fasting. Fasting, which lasted from two to six days before the event, meant not eating meat, salt, and chili peppers and other spices and not drinking beer. The Incas also refrained from sexual activity during this period.

The ceremonial rituals varied. They often took place in the plaza of Incan cities or in nearby fields or hills. The priests sometimes brought out the images of Viracocha, Inti, and Illapa. In Cuzco, at such times, the royal mummies were also put on display. Priests offered sacrifices, which occasionally required several hundred llamas. Many of these ceremonies ended with the burial of figures made from gold, silver, and seashells, plus the burning of carved wooden statues dressed in fine cloth. After the rituals were completed, the Incas danced, sang, ate, drank, and recounted high points of Incan history.

Incas offer a bowl of liqueur to the sun god Inti during one of their many ceromonies.

The Ceremonies of War

The Incas also had ceremonies for times of war. Archaeologist John Hyslop comments:

> Many rituals were associated with military activities. . . . Rituals and divinations guided and accompanied almost every step taken before, during, and after a military campaign. Portable sacred objects were carried to war. Rites were performed and offerings made to strengthen the Inkas' efforts as well as to diminish those of the enemy.[44]

At the beginning of a war, the priests at Cuzco sacrificed wild birds and llamas before the stone of war, a *huaca* that sat in the main plaza. The llamas had not been fed for days, and diviners examined the remains. If the dead animals' hearts had shrunk, it was a sign that the hearts of the enemy would grow weak and faint. Such ritual boosted the morale of Incan soldiers, who enforced the emperor's will when other methods failed.

CHAPTER SIX

SOLDIERS AND ENGINEERS

The Inca army was the chief tool for expanding the empire. It was also an important safeguard against threats from without and from within the imperial domains. The army's effectiveness was enhanced by the network of roads that the Incas built. Incan engineering, however, not only served to aid military control of the empire but also provided its own form of control of the imperial population.

Organization of the Army

The smallest unit in the Incan army had ten soldiers under the leadership of a Guardian of Ten, the equivalent of a modern-day sergeant. The Guardian of Ten saw to it that his men were armed, supplied, and trained.

Five of these ten-man units were assembled under the command of a Guardian of Fifty, who supervised the unit leaders under him by making regular inspections. Increasingly larger army sections led to divisions of one hundred, one thousand, twenty-five hundred, and five thousand soldiers.

Guardians of Ten and Fifty were commoners, who like their men were fulfilling their *mit'a* obligation. Commanders above these ranks were *curacas* and Incan aristocrats, the latter often being career army officers. The

The massive and skilled Inca army was the chief tool in expanding the empire.

highest-ranking general was the chief of the army and was chosen by the emperor and the imperial prefects. He was generally a brother or an uncle of the Sapa Inca, but was always a relative of the royal family. The emperor, of course, was the head of the army, as he was the head of both the government and the state religion.

Farmers and Warriors

The empire had very few troops on duty during peacetime. In fact, the only full-time soldiers were professional officers and the Sapa Inca's personal guard, which numbered a few thousand. Of the rest of the army, Davies notes, "the ordinary soldiers were . . . farmers who were liable for military service . . . ,

MOUNTAIN FORTRESS

The largest Incan military post so far discovered is Pambamarca, located on a mountain about twenty miles northeast of Quito, Ecuador. John Hyslop, in his *Inka Settlement Planning*, provides the following description of the complex.

> The highest and most central part of the Pambamarca complex is dominated by a massive installation . . . with five increasingly higher levels sustained [supported] by concentric walls. . . . The walls of this and other units are made of rough stone blocks quarried nearby. . . .
>
> Many doorways are found in the concentric walls. . . . The remains of at least two dozen buildings, all apparently rectangular, are found within the walls. . . .
>
> Running just to the north of Unit 1 is a trench with two walls on either side. It connects Unit 1 with Units 6, 11, and probably 13.
>
> [Unit 2] has three concentric walls. . . . There is no evidence of buildings. Unit 3 is lower and still simpler, with one concentric wall. The wall surrounds a rock outcrop [rock projecting from the ground]. Unit 4, the smallest in the complex, consists of only two concentric walls with no visible buildings. It rests directly north of an ancient road. . . . Units 4 and 5 may have controlled transit [travel on the road].
>
> Unit 5 . . . is a massive installation. . . . Two outer walls at right angles indicate that it was probably rectangular. Outside of the main walls farther to the north there is a rock outcrop surrounded by three walls on the west and steep cliffs on the east. Two concentric walls . . . make up the . . . southern part of [Unit 5]. . . .There are several doors in the outer wall. . . . Traces of . . . eighty buildings are found in the center of the unit.

Fortresses like these were placed throughout the Incan Empire to protect cities and towns.

rather than warriors with no other occupation as in a modern standing army."[45]

In addition to the small corps of professionals and the vast body of reserves, the empire had a group of semiregular soldiers. These latter staffed the fortresses that were placed throughout the empire and along its frontier. The forts generally sat atop hills overlooking cities and towns. Baudin writes:

> These strongholds . . . allowed their occupants to endure a prolonged siege. They formed small townships, with houses and cultivated terraces, and they were self-supporting, at least for a certain length of time. . . . These strongholds exist today in a ruined state and in many areas [that once were part of the Inca Empire]. . . . Their mission was to break the thrust of invaders and give the imperial armies time to mobilize. An invasion . . . from the eastern forests had miscarried [failed] against such defenses [in the early 1500s].[46]

The inhabitants of these forts were full-time residents but not full-time soldiers. They and their families, who also resided in the forts, lived and farmed in the same way as did commoners all over the empire. They took up their weapons only when attacked.

These garrison folk were generally not native to the regions in which they served, particularly those at frontier posts. They were resettled loyalists, and their orders were to make the forts their permanent homes, which they did.

The Coming of War

When war threatened, the imperial government put out a call to the provinces for enough *mit'a* commoners between the ages of twenty-five and fifty to fill the ranks. Each province then sent to Cuzco, or to some other designated point, a body of troops under the command of a *curaca* general. The final assembled army numbered between 70,000 and 250,000 soldiers, depending on the nature of the crisis.

The period of service for these troops could be quite lengthy, even stretching into years. Imperial officials often assigned other *mit'a* laborers to work the household land of soldiers on extended campaigns.

Reaching the Battlefield

The army was a colorful assemblage. Many warriors wore headdresses and their regional costume, decorating their shoulders and chest with feathers. Officers sported jewels and wore plumes on their helmets.

To reach the scene of battle required long marches, particularly to the frontiers, which were hundreds of miles, sometimes a thousand or more, from Cuzco. Common soldiers and most officers walked, while generals—and the emperor when he personally led the army—rode on litters. The litter was a platform to which poles were attached. On the platform was a stool for the rider. Sometimes an overhead canopy provided protection from the sun.

Four soldiers carried each litter, even into battle. Indeed, the emperor remained on his litter, surrounded by a thousand of his bodyguards, throughout the entire contest.

The marching order of the Incan army was by ethnic groups. The newest imperial subjects led the column. Those groups who had been in the empire longest, and were consequently considered the most trustworthy and loyal, were placed closest to the generals and the emperor, who brought up the rear.

Provisions came out of the state warehouses. While in the central provinces, the army was generally able to camp each night near towns and cities with storehouses. Here, food was distributed directly from storage to the troops. When the army reached the borderlands of the empire and beyond, their supplies were carried to them by llama trains.

Battle Goals

The Incas' battle plans were straightforward. First, the soldiers were to capture the enemy's chief leaders and any of their foes' *huacas* that had been brought to the battlefield.

Accomplishing these goals depended largely on the Incas overwhelming their opponents with sheer numbers. As soon as battle was joined, the conflict turned into a free-for-all of thousands of small hand-to-hand fights, where numbers counted even more than skill with weapons.

On the Battlefield

When the Incas finally confronted the enemy, they advanced to the accompaniment of drums, tambourines, and bone flutes. Trumpets made from clay or large seashells were used as signals. The warriors also sang and shouted. Sometimes officers and men alike painted their faces to frighten the enemy. Both noise and paint were designed to unnerve the opposition.

The Incan generals sometimes divided their forces into thirds and then had one division attack the enemy while keeping the remaining warriors hidden. After fighting began, the other two units would rush in and attack their opponent's rear from either side. At other times, Incan generals hit an enemy's weak point with a large number of Incan soldiers, splitting the opposing army in half. The fragmented foe was then surrounded and overcome.

Frequently, the enemy fell back to an easily defended position, such as the top of a hill or a fort. If possible, the Incas would set fire to scrub grass surrounding the enemy soldiers and burn them out. Otherwise, particularly with a fortress, the Incan warriors either would storm the stronghold, overrunning the defenders, or would set up a siege and wait for their foe to run out of food and water.

Weapons

The Incan army was armed with a variety of weapons. Customarily, troops similarly armed fought together. As the Incan force neared the enemy, warriors with slings hurled egg-sized stones with great force. At the same time, archers added arrows to the fray.

When the two sides finally closed, Incan soldiers rushed forward, swinging clubs and axes. A favorite club had a multipointed stone or piece of metal fastened to its end. The heads of the battle-axes were stone or copper. Additionally, some warriors threw small, dartlike spears, while others thrust at enemy warriors with longer spears.

Armor and Helmets

For protection, each soldier carried on his arm a round or square shield. Made of wood, these shields were covered with either metal or deerskin, over which was stretched a cloth bearing a painted or woven design. A second shield made of cotton or palm slats hung down each warrior's back.

Protection in battle was also provided by quilted cotton suits and wooden or cotton helmets. Copper, silver, and gold disks worn front and back and indicating rank offered further protection.

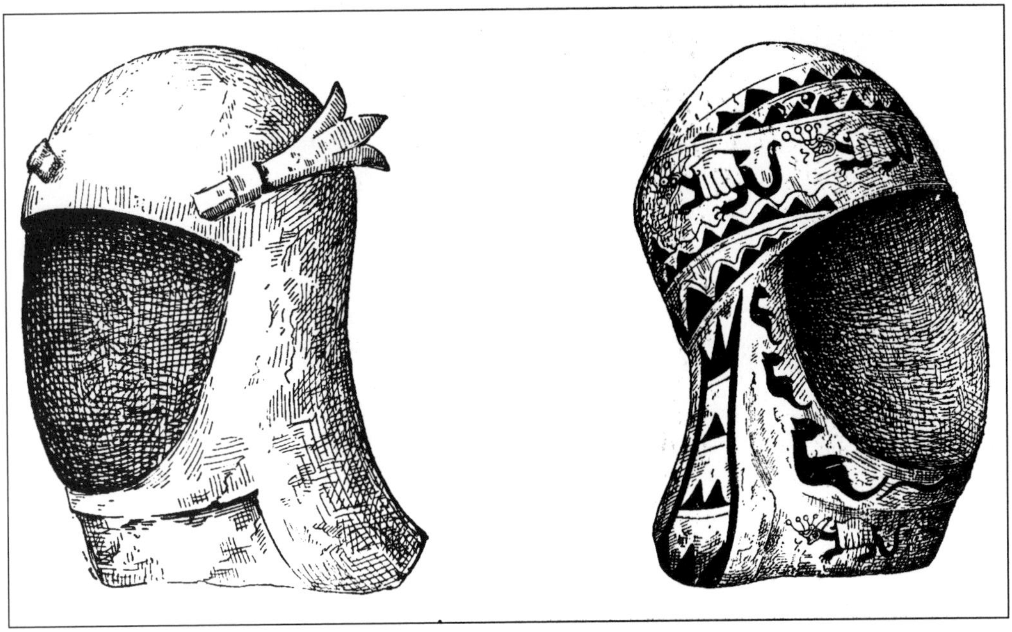

Incan soldiers wore either cotton or wooden helmets during battle.

Victory

Except for important leaders, the Incas did not take prisoners during battle. The idea was to kill as many of the enemy as possible. After the battle, Incan soldiers often made drums out of the skins of the dead enemy and flutes out of their bones.

Surviving enemy warriors, however, were not mistreated. Along with thousands of women and children from the defeated land, the prisoners were marched to Cuzco by the Incas to be shown off in a triumphant victory parade. The defeated warriors were then made to lie on their bellies while the emperor walked across their backs. Then most of the captives were released and allowed to return home. The empire wanted workers, not dead prisoners.

The emperor did order the execution or sacrifice of the most important enemy leaders. Many of these prisoners died in underground cells filled with hungry predators or venomous snakes.

The Spoils of War

The Sapa Inca gave unmarried captive women as gifts to his officers. To these aristocrats, the Incan ruler also handed out promotions and special privileges, such as the right to ride in a litter or sit on a stool.

Imperial gifts to common soldiers were also usual. They were offered in exchange for service in a dangerous enterprise. The sixteenth-century Spanish chronicler Juan de Betanzos wrote that the emperor Topa Inca "had all his soldiers assemble. . . . Wishing to pay them for the services they had rendered to him, . . . he did great favors for all of them, by giving them many women, valuables, and livestock, all of which had been taken as spoils from the enemy."[47]

Keys to Victory

The Incas won their wars because their army was large and well equipped. Further, their strategy and tactics, though simple, combined with competent leadership to make an effective fighting force.

Equally important to the success of the Incan army was that it could move efficiently to reach enemies and that it could keep itself easily supplied. These feats were possible because of the extensive road system that crisscrossed the Inca Empire.

The Roads

Through the course of their century of development, the Incas built fourteen thousand miles of roads. Two main roads ran north and south. One was in the highlands and stretched from northern Ecuador to Argentina. The second ran along the coast from the Ecuador-Peru border south into Chile. A network of roads branched from these trunk lines, connecting them and all the major cities of the empire, as well as leading to the imperial borders. The roads also ran to important shrines and holy sites.

Because the Incas did not have the wheel and thus no rolling vehicles, the roads were designed for foot travel and llama pack trains. Their width could vary considerably. In places, they were eighty feet wide, while in others they shrank to no more than a footpath. In places, they went straight up and down slopes, and in others curved gently around hills. To enable travelers to mount very steep slopes, the roads were designed as a series of steps.

Whole sections of raised roadbeds, retaining walls, and paved surfaces are still found in

ROADWAY

The Incan roads were the lifeline of the empire. Here, from *History of the Inca Empire*, the seventeenth-century Jesuit Bernabe Cobo, who lived most of his adult life in Peru, describes one of the roads that led up into the Andes.

> This road of . . . the sierra [mountains] and broken land was made by hand with much work and skill. If it passed through hillsides with cliffs and slabs of rock, a narrow path, only wide enough for one person leading a llama . . ., was dug in the boulder itself, and this type of construction did not run very far, but as soon as the boulder or slab of rock was passed, the road widened again. On some rugged slopes where the road could not be made across the middle of the hillside, strong steps were made of flat stones. . . . Across all the other . . . slopes, the road was . . . leveled off and ten or twelve feet wide. Where the slope was very steep, there was a wall of . . . stone . . . , and inside it was filled up with earth so that it was made even and perfectly level . . . ; in other places, on the upper side [of the slope], they had a wall made of stone without mortar . . . that would hold back the earth and rocks that rolled down from above, so that the road would not be blocked. . . . Where there was some ravine or narrow gorge that cut off the road [if not too deep], walls were also made from below and built up to the level of the road.

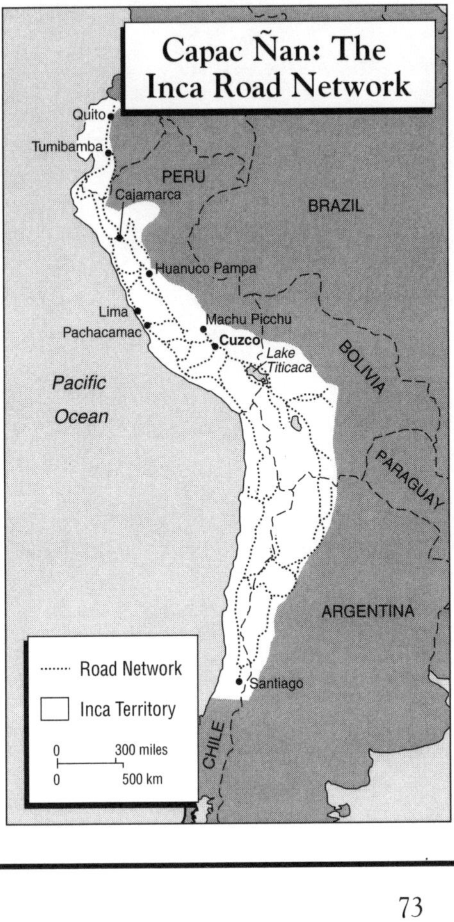

the Andean region, making the Inca road system the largest archaeological relic in South America. One such section runs along the mountain slopes between the ruins of Machu Picchu and another Incan town. In places, it is paved with flat stones; in others, it becomes steps hollowed out of the mountainside. Part of this road sits on earth piled high and packed against the mountain. This raised roadbed is held in place by twelve-foot-high walls. One segment even passes through a tunnel, which was made by enlarging a natural fissure in the rock.

Bridges

To cross highland rivers, which were deep, fast flowing, and often at the bottom of canyons, the Incas built bridges. Ropes crossed the river and anchored to wooden towers. Suspended from the ropes was a wooden walkway. The regular replacement of the ropes kept a number of these bridges in operation well into the nineteenth century. In fact, Andeans to this day can still throw such a bridge across a chasm when needed.

In the coastal lowlands, where riverbanks were lower and the water flowed more slowly,

The Incas built rope bridges across fast flowing rivers and canyons.

Tambos—small settlements along Incan roads—offered food and lodging for weary travelers.

stone and wooden bridges spanned the rivers. A few floating bridges also existed, their walkways kept afloat by huge bundles of dried reed.

Messengers and Travelers

Walking an Incan road required official permission. For the most part, roads were restricted to the military and those on state business. The general population normally kept off them, except when as *mit'a* workers, they were required to build or repair the roads. Thus, the roads remained clear and open to official traffic.

Imperial roads allowed for speedy delivery of messages and news to any point in the empire. Threats of invasion or rebellion, for instance, reached Cuzco via messengers running these roads. The response was an army marching back along the same route. Strings of runners also carried orders or quipu from Cuzco to provincial capitals.

Messengers were posted at way stations that lined the roads at intervals of a mile and a half. At each station were several small huts in which two runners lived. While one slept, the other awaited messages, which he would carry to the next way station. In this fashion, messages traveled 125 to 150 miles a day. As an example, a royal order from Cuzco could reach Quito in Ecuador, some 800 miles away, in five or six days.

Along the road were also small settlements, called *tambos*, which provided inns for other road travelers. Imperial officials, either on inspection trips or being transferred to the provinces, were among these travelers. The emperor himself occasionally toured the empire, and his party would shelter in the *tambos*. Likewise, the army would stop at the road settlements, but would pitch tents because of their numbers.

Other travelers transported corn, coca, metal, textiles, feathers, and luxury goods. This traffic was either headed to Cuzco for the use of the emperor and the Incan aristocracy or on its way as imperial gifts to important *curacas*.

Symbols of Authority

The roads were more than a communication and transportation system. They were also a symbol of Incan power. Hyslop observes that

> to conquered populations throughout the Inka empire, the roads were an omnipresent [universal] symbol of the power and authority of the Inka state. There were probably very few individuals subject to the Inka state who had never seen an Inka road, even though many of these individuals had . . . rarely seen an actual Inka from the region around Cuzco.[48]

Nor were the roads the only constructions that announced imperial might. Incan public architecture in general was monumental in scale and size. It was meant to impress, to awe, to overwhelm, leading archaeologists Graciano Gasparini and Luise Margolies to call it "architecture of power."[49]

In the Incan capital of Cuzco, Coricancha, the main temple, had a perimeter of twelve hundred feet. On its exterior walls were plates of gold that caught and reflected sunlight.

Atop a hill at the city's north end was the Sacsahuaman, a massive structure whose walls were made of stones measuring thirteen feet high. The Spanish estimated that the Sacsahuaman could hold as many as five thousand people.

The purpose of the Sacsahuaman is something of a mystery. Because of the structure's size and its high placement, the first Spanish to see the building thought it was a fortress. Chroniclers, such as Pedro de Cieza de León and Garcilaso de la Vega, mentioned that the Sacsahuaman was used for religious ceremonies, which they fail to describe. The Spanish also wrote that many of the rooms were filled with weapons, pottery, jewelry, and clothing, leading some modern scholars to speculate that the Sacsahuaman may have been part storehouse.

The construction of the many roads and public buildings served the empire in another way as well. It kept imperial subjects hard at work; some of the building projects used up to thirty thousand laborers at a time. Between tending their fields and their labor for the state, commoners had little time for recreation, let alone plotting rebellion.

Fine Masonry

Size was not the only feature of imperial public buildings. The walls of these structures were examples of the remarkable Incan stonework. The stones fit so tightly against one another that a knife blade cannot slip between them. Archaeologists call such work fine masonry.

Incan stonemasons, stoneworking specialists, carefully chipped away at rocks dragged from quarries. They used bronze chisels and stone hammers to shape the edges so that a rock could nestle among its neighbors. From time to time, other workers lifted the stone into place so that the mason could check its fit. Then the *mit'a* laborers would heave the rock back out and down for the mason to continue his work. The last stage of creating the fit required hours of tedious rubbing of the stone's edges with sand and water. Bankes notes, "Although no mortar was used on the exterior face of the wall, in the interior the stones were rarely perfectly fitted and the cracks were filled with mud."[50]

In the Cuzco area, the ruins of fine masonry buildings are common. They are less so in other cities in the empire. Unless the imperial officials were constructing a city from scratch, they contented themselves with adding a few government buildings and temples to already existing urban centers. These new structures marked the city as Incan property.

Cuzco

The identity of the Incan engineers, like many other aspects of the Inca Empire, is unknown. Whoever they were, they were skilled at their jobs. Civil engineer Kenneth R. Wright and archaeologist Alfredo Valencia Zegarra point out that "the well-preserved remains of Machu Picchu show that they had an advanced understanding of such principles as urban planning, . . . drainage, and durable construction methods."[51]

Cuzco was the crown jewel of Incan urban planning and probably the largest imperial

INCAN CONSTRUCTION

By studying surviving Incan buildings, archaeologists have learned how the Incas erected the walls of these structures. In *Machu Picchu: A Civil Engineering Marvel*, Kenneth R. Wright and Alfredo Valencia Zegarra describe this process, which began with a trench dug deep into the ground.

> The Inca technique for constructing wall foundations started with the careful placement of smaller rocks in the excavation [trench] bottom to create a firm bedding. The rocks became larger as the foundation rose nearer the ground. A typical wall was . . . 2.6 feet thick at the groundline. . . . In some instances, the Incan engineers selected a . . . granite rock [that was part of the ground] . . . for their foundation . . . , which was first shaped to provide a ledge or platform for [the foundation]. Examples include the Temple of the Sun [in Machu Picchu]. . . .
>
> In wall construction, the building stones were alternately placed in the wall lengthwise and then crosswise for stability. . . . Many of the stones have top and bottom indentations that helped fit them together in a nesting manner. Corner stones nearly always have such indentations to provide additional stability. . . . Mortar consisting of clay and earth mixed with small stones was used in many of the walls. . . .
>
> At Machu Picchu at least 18 different stone wall types and patterns range from the finest carving and shaping to the roughest type of permanent construction for use in agricultural terraces. There are even examples of rough, temporary construction stone walls used as an inclined plane for moving large blocks upward.

city with a population of one hundred thousand. By tradition, Pachacuti Inca Yupanqui had designed the Incan capital, even pacing off the building sites himself. According to the Spanish, Pachacuti had laid the city out in the shape of a puma, or mountain lion. The head was the Sacsahuaman, and the tail, a narrow section of the city built between two rivers, the Huatanay and the Tullumayo. To give the geography a more tail-like appearance, the Incas straightened out the beds of the rivers.

At Cuzco's center were two plazas, divided from each other by a third river, the Saphy. The eastern plaza was the main city square and was floored with sand brought from the beaches of the Pacific.

In the city's heart was also the Coricancha, the Inca's palace, the homes of Incas-by-blood, and the workshop of the Chosen Women. Surrounding the city's core were agricultural fields. Then came residential neighborhoods, which housed visiting *curacas* as well as artisans and other resettled workers. At Cuzco's edge were the homes of the Incas-by-privilege.

Other Cities

The Incas used Cuzco as a model for other cities. Nonetheless, Incan engineers were not slaves to its plan.

In Cuzco, for example, the central streets formed a grid—that is, the streets crossed each other at right angles. In the outer sec-

Archeologists believe that Machu Picchu—the ruins shown here—might have been a religious retreat for the emperor.

tions, the streets radiated out like the spokes of a wheel. In other Incan cities, designers used one pattern or the other, but not both. Additionally, where plazas were found in the heart of Cuzco, they were placed to the side or at the end of other towns.

Machu Picchu

With Machu Picchu, Incan engineers built a very specialized and unique city. Located fifty miles northwest of Cuzco, this city lacked many features normally found in Incan settlements. Archaeologist Karen Wise writes that missing are

> storage silos . . . and administrative buildings as might be expected for a center of state administration. The city lacks the features of a seat of government or of a town of mainly economic or military importance. Although the agricultural products of the area surrounding Machu Picchu—coca and other crops—may have been important to the empire, the city itself did not function . . . as an agricultural . . . center. Rather it was probably a retreat, . . . where the emperor went to engage in religious or other activities away from his capital city.[52]

Incan engineers provided the city with many points from which the sun could be observed. Also, they laid out the city so that it had an excellent view of three holy mountains nearby. Archaeologists believe that these features support the idea that Machu Picchu was designed as a religious retreat for the emperor.

At the beginning of the sixteenth century, the Inca Empire appeared strong and vigorous, its people and its enemies seemingly under control. Its roads and public buildings were a constant reminder of the Incas' might and power. Yet, that might and power was about to be challenged by a foe unlike any this Andean people had ever known.

Chapter Seven

The Fall of the Incas

The last years of the Inca Empire's existence was a stormy period, marked by disease, civil war, and invasion. Under these hammer blows of misfortune, the empire crumpled. Its collapse was hastened by its subject people grasping the opportunity to break free of Incan control. In the end, Incas and non-Incas alike would find themselves under new rulers, the Spanish.

Disease

Around 1527, an epidemic struck the Inca Empire. When it hit Cuzco and its surrounding territory, it claimed an estimated two hundred thousand lives, among them the empress. The emperor Huayna Capac, who was in Quito, also came down with the disease and died.

The deadliness of the disease indicates that it was probably European—smallpox, typhus, or measles. The peoples of the Americas had no immunity to these foreign illnesses and died in huge numbers when exposed to them. Whichever disease ravaged the Inca Empire, it may have worked its way south from Spanish-controlled Central America, infecting tribe after tribe until some infected individual crossed into the Inca Empire.

The Rivals

With the death of Huayna Capac, the empire was without a leader. On his deathbed, the emperor had named his son Ninan Cuyuchi his successor. However, if the signs did not favor Ninan Cuyuchi, then his eldest son Huascar was to become Sapa Inca. Ninan Cuyuchi soon died in the epidemic, and Huascar became emperor.

Both Ninan Cuyuchi and Huascar were sons of Huayna Capac's official wife. However, the dead emperor's favorite among his sons was Atahuallpa, the son of a secondary wife. Atahuallpa's birth barred him from becoming emperor, so Huayna left him Ecuador to rule.

Technically, Atahuallpa was still subject to Huascar, and he sent messengers to the new emperor pledging his loyalty. Nevertheless, Atahuallpa stayed in Quito, despite commands from his brother to return to Cuzco.

At Atahuallpa's back was his father's army, with which he had served. Years of fighting along the northern imperial border had battle-hardened these troops and made them confident of their ability to win any armed contest. Tough veterans all, they were completely loyal to Atahuallpa.

No matter the legal status of Atahuallpa, Huascar was afraid that his half brother had his sights set on the Incan throne. Indeed,

Atahuallpa began to act like an emperor, for according to Edward Hyams and George Ordish, "[Atahuallpa] began . . . to surround himself with the pomp and ceremony suitable to a Sapa Inca."[53]

The War of the Two Brothers

Tension between the brothers rose until Huascar sent an imperial army north in 1529 to capture his brother. Raw recruits, fulfilling their *mit'a,* made up the emperor's army. They were no match for Atahuallpa's veterans, who in two days of fighting killed some fifteen thousand and sent the rest running south in panic.

This battle was only the first in what would be a particularly vicious civil war, known as the War of the Two Brothers. Both sides burned down towns and killed those loyal to the other side. Atahuallpa was particularly vengeful, having the population of whole towns killed as he watched.

Atahuallpa declared himself emperor after defeating his half brother Huascar.

Atahuallpa's army captures Huascar during the War of the Two Brothers.

Atahuallpa Victorious

Finally, in 1532, Huascar was captured in a battle just outside Cuzco. Atahuallpa was in Quito, but when he heard news of the victory, he declared himself the sole ruler of the empire. Because he was not the legal heir to the throne, he decided to eliminate anyone who might be.

Thus, on Atahuallpa's orders, the victorious generals at Cuzco hunted down and killed all of Huascar's uncles, nephews, and cousins. They even killed quipu readers and servants in an attempt to erase any memory of Huascar's reign. Last, they made the deposed monarch watch as they slaughtered his wives and children, whose bodies were then impaled on wooden stakes. Huascar, his wife, and his mother were spared temporarily until Atahuallpa could arrive from Quito, because the victor wished to watch the torture and execution of these three.

The Strangers

In the north, Atahuallpa set off for Cuzco. However, he stopped first in the Peruvian highland city of Cajamarca. For some time, he had been receiving reports about a band of bearded strangers who had recently landed on Peru's north coast. Curious to see these men, the new emperor invited them to meet him at Cajamarca.

The strangers were conquistadors, Spanish adventurers. As their name suggested, they were conquerors, and their goal was nothing less than the conquest of the Inca Empire.

Francisco Pizarro

Commanding this Spanish expedition was Francisco Pizarro. Born around 1475, Pizarro

WARM WELCOME AT TUMBES

In 1527, Francisco Pizarro landed at Tumbes, a northern port for the Inca Empire. Unlike the later expedition of conquest, relations between the local population and the Spanish remained cordial, as sixteenth-century chronicler Pedro de Cieza de León recounts in his *Discovery and Conquest of Peru*.

> Ten or twelve balsas [rafts] were prepared—replete [filled] with food and fruit, many jugs of water and *chicha* and fish and a lamb [llama] that the virgins of the temple [Chosen Women] gave to take to them [the Spanish]. The Indians went to the ship with all this without guile [trickery] or malice, but rather with joy and pleasure to see such people. . . .
>
> Among the Indians was an *orejón* [Incan aristocrat], . . . who said to the captain [Pizarro] that they could safely come on land without being harmed and provision themselves with water and whatever they needed. . . .
>
> The captain ordered that they should give him [the Incan aristocrat] food and . . . wine, and he gazed at that brew, which seemed to him better and tastier than theirs. When he was leaving the captain gave him an iron axe, which . . . pleased him, esteeming [prizing] it more than if they had given him one hundred times more gold than it weighed. And he [Pizarro] further gave . . . a few pearls . . . ; for the *cacique principal* [senior *curaca*] he gave one sow, one boar, four hens, and one rooster. . . .
>
> When the cacique saw the presents, he appreciated them more than I can express, and all came to see the sow and the boar and the hens, delighting in hearing the rooster crow.

was the illegitimate son of a minor Spanish nobleman. Almost nothing is known about his childhood, although legend has it that he tended pigs for a time. He apparently received no formal education because he was illiterate.

Lack of education did not keep Pizarro from being ambitious. James Lockhart comments that "Francisco Pizarro . . . bore a good name and was imbued [filled] with the ambitions that accompanied it, yet his upbringing was more plebeian [common] than noble."[54]

In 1502, the young Spaniard sought his fortune, like many others, by going to the New World. Over the next twenty years, he campaigned in Colombia, took part in the first European expedition to see the Pacific Ocean, and served as mayor of Panama City.

First Contact

In 1522, a Spanish soldier returned to Panama with gold jewelry he had gotten from a tribe in western Colombia. Pizarro decided that he wished to find the source of that gold and set out with an expedition in 1524 to explore the Pacific coast of Colombia. Three years of hardship brought him nothing until a ship coming to relieve his party captured a balsa wood raft that had a rich cargo of gold and silver. Such rafts were commonly used by the Incas to transport goods along the coast.

Excited by the news, Pizarro convinced the ship's captain to head further south, where they discovered the Incan city of Tumbes. Pizarro and his party landed and were awed by the lavish display of Incan wealth they saw. Possibly, they also infected the local population with the disease that would soon kill many in the empire.

Captain General

Pizarro returned north to assemble another expedition, this time with the purpose of invading and conquering the Inca Empire. He then sailed to Spain, where he convinced King Charles to appoint him captain general of Peru, even though it was the home of a flourishing civilization. Joining Pizarro on his return were his three half brothers, Gonzalo, Hernando, and Juan.

On May 16, 1532, Pizarro was back at Tumbes. This time, he had the men, the equipment, and the horses to capture the city, but it was not necessary. Tumbes was a burned-out shell, having been torched during the War of the Two Brothers.

For the first time, Pizarro learned about the Incan civil war and immediately began planning ways to exploit the chaos and bitterness left by the conflict. He sent parties out to recruit allies from among the locals, who now saw their chance to break free of Incan rule. Rostworowski observes:

> The majority of the great Andean lords [the *curacas*] were only waiting for the opportunity to shake off the Inca presence. . . . It is not surprising that the ethnic chiefs saw the Spaniards as allies who would help them recover their past independence. . . . They could not know, or guess, that behind the soldiers of Pizarro stood the menacing presence of a country desirous of conquering the New World. . . . It appears likely that Pizarro understood well the situation created by the Spanish presence, and took advantage of the opportunity to offer his self-interested support to the cause of the local lords of the country.[55]

Francisco Pizarro planned to conquer the Inca Empire for its silver and gold.

To Cajamarca

Despite Pizarro's activities, Atahuallpa did not appear to see the invaders as a threat. There were too few of them, and they were too far from reinforcements. On the other hand, he had an army that numbered in the tens of thousands and that had just won a great victory. Thus, Atahuallpa extended his invitation to Pizarro, even going so far as to send gifts of gold jewelry and embroidered cloth to the conquistador leader.

Pizarro decided to gamble by accepting the Sapa Inca's invitation. Knowing that he might be riding into a trap, he and 168 men, with 67 on horses, set off for Cajamarca. The Spanish were nervous and suspicious, not understanding why they were being allowed to penetrate deep into the empire. Still, their fears did not dim their awe on first encountering Incan roads, and they appreciated the ease with which they could now move up into the mountains toward Cajamarca. They also prized the food and hospitality they received at *tambos*, where they stopped each night.

At Cajamarca

When on November 15 Pizarro and his expedition rode into the Cajamarca Valley, all their fears resurfaced. Below them, they were stunned to see the tents of an army numbering at least fifty thousand. Later, one conquistador, Juan Ruiz de Arce, would admit that "until then, we had never seen anything like this [the Incan army] in the Indies [the New World]. It filled all our Spaniards with fear and confusion."[56]

Hiding their fear, the Spanish followed guides down and into the city. The entire town was empty except for a handful of people left to act as servants for the conquistadors. The Spanish took up residence in buildings on the triangular-shaped city plaza.

Evening the Odds

The conquistadors were vastly outnumbered by the Incas, but the Spanish were far from helpless. Albert Marrin points out that the

> conquistadors . . . had the most advanced weapons of the age. Their bodies were protected by suits of armor made of steel. . . . On their heads each wore a steel helmet. . . . Spanish infantry might also wear shirts of chain mail, . . . [which] could turn away any stone- or copper-tipped spear. . . . Each man wore a sword and a dagger at his belt. . . . The Spanish sword . . . was made of Toledo steel said to be the strongest and most flexible in the world.[57]

In addition, the Spanish had cannons, guns, and crossbows.

And the conquistadors had horses, something the Incas had never seen before. These were warhorses that weighed one thousand pounds and could gallop at twenty miles an hour. A cavalry charge with such horses could be stopped but not with any weapons the Incas possessed. Additionally, the horse made an excellent fighting platform, giving its rider height from which to swing a sword downward in a powerful blow. The force of such a blow could split the steel of chain mail, and the Incan soldiers had no armor stronger than quilted cotton.

Trap

The conquistadors had a chance to use their superior weaponry the very next day. Pizarro invited Atahuallpa to come visit the Spanish

A conquistador rides a warhorse, which the Incas had not seen before the Spanish introduced them to Peru.

in Cajamarca. The emperor accepted. When the Sapa Inca arrived, he was surrounded by several thousand Incan aristocrats. Only a few, however, were armed, and only with slings and clubs. The army's warriors waited outside the city.

Pizarro's invitation was a trap, and after the emperor and his party were in the city plaza, the Spanish leader waved a white scarf. The conquistadors attacked. The lightly armed Incas went down under sword, gun, cannon, and horses' hooves. In a little over an hour, the conquistadors killed three thousand Incas but suffered no losses of their own. It was a massacre, but at its end, Pizarro held the emperor captive.

Ransom

By grabbing the head of the Incan state, Pizarro had control, at least temporarily, over the Incas. The Incan army could do nothing, would do nothing, as long as by their inaction they kept their emperor alive. To be sure of the army's good conduct, Pizarro had Atahuallpa order the warriors to surrender.

Atahuallpa, recovering from the shock of his capture, realized that what the Spanish wanted most was gold and silver. He promised to fill a room seventeen by twenty-two feet to a height of eight feet with gold objects and two adjacent rooms with silver if Pizarro would eventually release him. The conquistador leader readily agreed.

It took almost six months for the treasure to be gathered from Cuzco and other Incan cities. During that time, the Spanish allowed Atahuallpa to have his servants, his gold and silver dinner plates, and his constant change of clothes. He was also in communication with his generals and, while waiting for the rooms to be filled, sent word to his followers to kill Huascar, as well as the defeated man's wife and mother. The deed was soon done.

In the end, the emperor kept his promise to Pizarro. The rooms were filled with enough gold and silver vases, jars, benches, stools, and even a fountain to be worth today over $90 million. Samuel K. Lothrop writes that "it was an ancient custom in Spanish armies that a victorious general could select a single article from the spoils, apart from his share. . . . [Pizarro's] choice was a golden . . . litter, which . . . weighed . . . over 200 pounds."[58] The Spanish melted all the objects, including Pizarro's litter, down and recast them as ingots for easy transport.

The Death of Atahuallpa

Pizarro, however, did not keep his promise to Atahuallpa. The Sapa Inca remained a prisoner. Then, in July 1533, Pizarro had Atahuallpa executed, supposedly for plotting to kill the conquistadors. In reality, there was no plot, but it was a convenient fiction that allowed Pizarro to dispose of his captive.

Pizarro's reasons for killing the Incan leader have never been clear. Many of his own men, and later scholars, accused him of throwing away his only shield against the Incas, having gained nothing in return. However, Hyams and Ordish suggest that Pizarro believed

> it would be difficult, if not impossible, to continue keeping Atahuallpa a prisoner. . . . If a really determined effort were made to rescue the Sapa Inca it might succeed; it would at least succeed in killing a great many Spaniards of a very small company. . . . The Spanish leader had now seen . . . for himself the paralysis of the great [Incan] bureaucracy . . . when deprived of its head. It was true that the death of

THE CAPTURE OF ATAHUALLPA

In *Guns, Germs, and Steel: The Fates of Human Societies*, Jared Diamond reprints the following eyewitness account by Diego de Trujillo of Pizarro's seizure of the Incan emperor Atahuallpa.

> The governor [Pizarro] concealed his troops around the square, . . . dividing the cavalry into two portions. . . . In like manner he divided the infantry, he himself taking one part. . . . At the same time he ordered Pedro de Candia and two . . . infantrymen to go with trumpets to a small fort [building] in the plaza and to station themselves there with a small piece of artillery. When . . . Atahuallpa . . . had entered the plaza, the governor would give a signal . . . , after which they should start firing the gun, and the trumpets should sound, and at the sound of the trumpets the cavalry should dash out. . . .
>
> The armored Spanish troops . . . sallied out of their hiding places straight into the mass of . . . Indians. . . . We had placed rattles on the horses to terrify the Indians. The booming of the guns, the blowing of the trumpets, and the rattles . . . threw the Indians into panicked confusion. The Spaniards fell upon them and cut them to pieces. . . . The calvary rode them down, killing and wounding and following in pursuit. The infantry made so good an assault on those that remained that in short time most of them were put to the sword. . . .
>
> The governor himself . . . grabbed Atahuallpa's left arm . . . , but he could not pull Atahuallpa out of his litter because it was held so high. Although we killed the Indians who held the litter, others at once took their place. . . . Finally, . . . Spaniards on horseback . . . rushed upon the litter from one side, and with great effort, they heaved it over on its side. In that way Atahuallpa was captured.

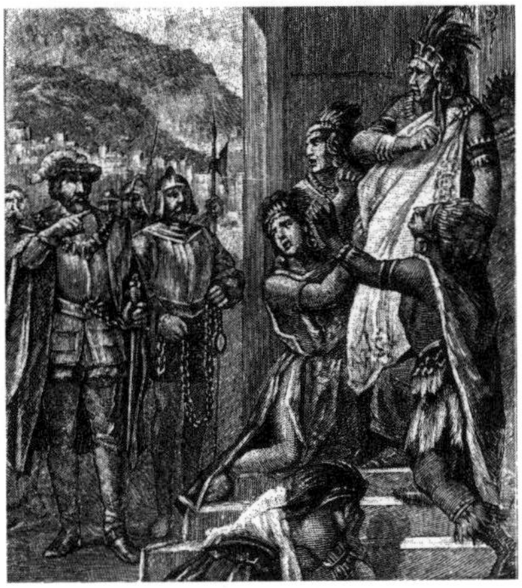

An artist's rendition of the capture of Atahuallpa. Pizarro's men eventually executed the Inca leader.

> Atahuallpa might set free certain generals . . . to take . . . hostile [action] . . . ; but their attacks would not be concerted [coordinated], they would soon be quarreling among themselves, and the more discontented provinces would refuse to accept their authority.[59]

Further, with Huascar and Atahuallpa dead and the imperial throne empty, Pizarro was free to find an emperor that he could control. For his imperial puppet, he chose another of Atahuallpa's brothers, Topa Huallpa. The conquistadors soon set off with their candidate for Cuzco.

To Cuzco

The Cuzco journey took two months and four battles. With Atahuallpa dead, his generals were free to attack the conquistadors, and they did so. Outside the city of Jauja, the Spanish came to a broad, shallow river. On the other bank stood ten thousand In-

LOOTING CUZCO

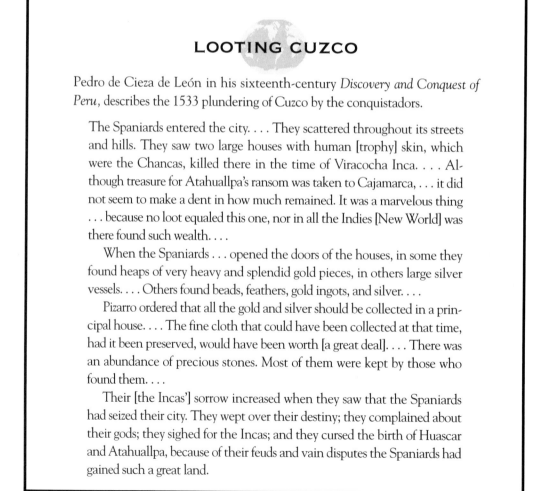

Pedro de Cieza de León in his sixteenth-century *Discovery and Conquest of Peru*, describes the 1533 plundering of Cuzco by the conquistadors.

> The Spaniards entered the city. . . . They scattered throughout its streets and hills. They saw two large houses with human [trophy] skin, which were the Chancas, killed there in the time of Viracocha Inca. . . . Although treasure for Atahuallpa's ransom was taken to Cajamarca, . . . it did not seem to make a dent in how much remained. It was a marvelous thing . . . because no loot equaled this one, nor in all the Indies [New World] was there found such wealth. . . .
>
> When the Spaniards . . . opened the doors of the houses, in some they found heaps of very heavy and splendid gold pieces, in others large silver vessels. . . . Others found beads, feathers, gold ingots, and silver. . . .
>
> Pizarro ordered that all the gold and silver should be collected in a principal house. . . . The fine cloth that could have been collected at that time, had it been preserved, would have been worth [a great deal]. . . . There was an abundance of precious stones. Most of them were kept by those who found them. . . .
>
> Their [the Incas'] sorrow increased when they saw that the Spaniards had seized their city. They wept over their destiny; they complained about their gods; they sighed for the Incas; and they cursed the birth of Huascar and Atahuallpa, because of their feuds and vain disputes the Spaniards had gained such a great land.

In an attempt to drive out the Spanish, Manco Inca and fifty thousand warriors laid siege to the city of Cuzco. This drawing depicts the chaos and violence that ensued.

can warriors. The battle was over quickly. The Spanish cavalry charged across the river and hit the Inca lines, shattering any resistance. Steel swords, crossbows, and guns forced the Incas to retreat. The conquistadors had similar success in the remaining battles they fought to reach Cuzco. The Spanish casualties were light, with only a few men and horses killed.

On November 15, 1533, exactly one year from their entrance into Cajamarca, Pizarro and his men rode into Cuzco. Here they watched as the new Inca emperor was crowned. However, this Sapa Inca was Manco Inca, a younger brother of Huascar, Topa Huallpa having died on the march to Cuzco. Manco had declared himself willing to work with the conquistadors. All he asked was that they help him destroy the rest of Atahuallpa's followers.

Resistance

The conquistadors' hold on the Inca Empire was far from complete or secure. They encountered heavy resistance when they invaded Ecuador, and even in Peru, which was their chief base of operation, they were plagued by a series of rebellions.

By 1536, after three years of watching his empire being looted, Manco Inca decided that the Spanish were more to be feared than Atahuallpa's supporters. He was also angered by the desire of Spanish priests to destroy the Incan religion and to replace it with Christianity.

Manco attacked Cuzco with fifty thousand warriors in an attempt to drive its new overlords out. He came close to succeeding, and he and his troops occupied the Sacsahuaman for over a year. But in the end, he was defeated. Again, one of the deciding factors was cavalry. Diamond writes that a "cavalry charge of 26 horsemen routed the best troops of Emperor Manco."[60] Forced to retreat to the eastern slopes of the Andes, Manco Inca set up a new, reduced Incan state.

The New Order

During this same period, Pizarro and the other conquistadors worked to strengthen their grip on Peru and the rest of the old empire. With Manco Inca's defection, they installed a new puppet emperor at Cuzco. The Spanish, however, kept more of the Inca Empire than the emperor. They continued the *mit'a* system, although they increased the amount of labor required. They also found it useful to retain Quechua as a means of communicating throughout their new domain.

One major change the Spanish made was to eliminate the exchange of goods for work. In its place, they introduced money. They also brought in wheat and other European crops, as well as cattle, sheep, and goats.

Continued Fighting

In 1535, Pizarro founded Lima, which became the capital of Peru. Over the next few years, he became entangled in a series of feuds with other conquistadors, open battle erupting at one point between the quarreling parties. Finally, in 1541, Pizarro was attacked and killed by his enemies. Supposedly, as he was dying, he drew the sign of the cross with his own blood and kissed it.

Meanwhile, from the eastern Andes, Manco Inca, and later his sons, launched a series of raids into Spanish territory. Their targets were often Spanish colonists who were flocking to Peru.

In 1565, Manco's son Sayri Topa helped plan a general Peruvian uprising. The plan failed, its only result being a harsh crackdown on native Andeans. Seven years later, the Spanish destroyed this last remnant of the Inca Empire when they captured and executed its final ruler, Topa Amaru.

Epilogue

The Incan Legacy

Puppet emperors would continue to sit in Cuzco for generations, but they were powerless, mere mouthpieces for the Spanish authorities. With the death of Topa Amaru in 1572, the Inca Empire ended. However, its legacy remains alive today around the world and specifically in the Andean region.

Contributions to the World

The Inca Empire ruled only in western South America, but its impact eventually extended far beyond its borders. It was Inca gold and silver that, in part, paid for much of the European Renaissance. Goodly portions of the money that poured into Europe from Spanish-held Peru went to pay architects, artists, writers, and musicians, whose work is still an important part of Western culture.

The Incas were also responsible for giving the world a number of popular foods. In fact, two of their major crops, corn and potatoes, are extremely important cash crops around the world. Additionally, it was from the Incas that today's world received tomatoes, several types of beans, chili peppers, peanuts, pineapples, sweet potatoes, and cashews.

Architecture and Art

Additionally, the Incas left the world a rich legacy of architecture and art. Their impressive fine masonry is visible at Machu Picchu, in the ruins around Cuzco, and at other sites in the Andes. The soundness of their buildings has allowed these structures to weather five centuries of earthquakes that have leveled more modern buildings.

Although much of the gold and silver jewelry, figures, containers, and the like were melted down by the conquistadors, some have survived, as have Incan textiles and pottery. These pieces reveal the skill of the artisans who made them. Further, their designs have been taken by modern Andean artists and melded with techniques from Europe and elsewhere to create something wholly new and original. In painting, for example, Western three-dimensional figures are often overlapped so that, in Incan fashion, their faces share a single pair of eyes.

Land and Family

The Incan legacy, of course, is strongest in the Andean region of South America. Stone-Miller writes that "despite the profound changes of the last 500 years, the Andean people have maintained a . . . vital continuity with their . . . past."[61] In western South America, it is the old home of the Incas, the Andes highlands, where that past is the most clearly seen. In addition to Spanish, people in the mountains still speak Quechua, which can be heard in markets and streets throughout the region. Many Andeans use the Incan language, rather than Spanish, in describing their relationships to other family members.

Despite the introduction of Western crops and animals, many farmers in the Andes prefer

The legacy of the Incan Empire still influences the Andean people today. Shown is a modern day Peruvian woman.

the old Incan standards: corn, beans, squash, and potatoes. They still eat guinea pigs and raise alpacas and llamas for their wool. In the more distant parts of the Andes, people still use the llama as a pack animal. Mules and horses may carry larger loads, but llamas are more surefooted.

Farming in the highlands is still done on fields that the Incas built or expanded. Also, as in Incan times, the produce of many farms is mostly for the use of the farmers and their families rather than for sale in town markets.

Ayllus still control land, both cropland and pasture, parceling it out to each household just as they did in Incan times. And, as their ancestors did, all the members of an Andean ayllu work to maintain the group's irrigation canals.

Religion

The old Incan religion is gone, at least as it was practiced under the Sapa Inca. However, many of its features have been folded into Catholicism. For instance, Christmas and the Incan festival Capac Raymi fall around the same time, and over time, elements of the Incan ritual, such as dancing, singing, and drinking *chicha*, merged with the Christian celebration.

Huacas still exist in the Andes. Various places, particularly mountains, are believed to be the dwelling places of spirits. Many Andeans see the major Catholic festival, Corpus Christi, as a chance to visit mountain *huacas* and make offerings of *chicha*. And the idea that Earth is still Pacha-Mama is common among the descendants of the Incas, perhaps because their homeland is still wracked by earthquakes and threatened by volcanoes.

In the end, the most important legacy of the Inca Empire is its continuing effect on the region it once ruled. Malpass puts it this way:

> Perhaps the most enduring legacy of the Incas is the extent of change they brought to the groups they conquered. It was the Incas' goal to . . . level the dramatic political and social differences that had existed between groups prior to the Inca expansion. To do this, they moved individuals and entire villages around the empire, breaking up larger societies and lumping smaller ones into administrative units of equal size. They introduced the Quechua language to their subjects, and it persists to this day. . . . The sense of common culture that millions of Andean people share today is more the result of the Incas' policies than those of the Spaniards. . . . Thus it is difficult to say that the Incas no longer exist; . . . Inca culture is very much alive today—although in a modified form. This heritage is the greatest tribute to the Incas' impact on western South America.[62]

Notes

Introduction: The Incan Civilization

1. Brian M. Fagan, *Kingdoms of Gold, Kingdoms of Jade: The Americas Before Columbus*. London: Thames and Hudson, 1991, p. 41.
2. Michael E. Moseley, *The Incas and Their Ancestors: The Archaeology of Peru*. London: Thames and Hudson, 1992, p. 7.
3. Michael A. Malpass, *Daily Life in the Inca Empire*. Westport, CT: Greenwood Press, 1996, p. xxi.
4. María Rostworowski de Diez Canseco, *History of the Inca Realm*, trans. Harry B. Iceland. Cambridge, England: Cambridge University Press, 1999, p. 47.

Chapter 1: Before the Incas

5. William H. Prescott, *History of the Conquest of Peru*. New York: Heritage Press, 1847, pp. 4–5.
6. Craig Morris and Adriana von Hagen, *The Inka Empire and Its Andean Origins*. New York: Abbeville Press, 1993, p. 12.
7. Moseley, *The Incas and Their Ancestors*, p. 43.
8. Ann Kendall, *Everyday Life of the Incas*. London: B.T. Batsford, 1973, p. 152.
9. Edward P. Lanning, *Peru Before the Incas*. Englewood Cliffs, NJ: Prentice-Hall, 1967, p. 96.
10. Malpass, *Daily Life in the Inca Empire*, p. 17.
11. Pedro de Cieza de León, *The Incas*, ed. Victor Wolfgang von Hagen, trans. Harriet de Onis. Norman: University of Oklahoma Press, 1959, pp. 282–83.
12. Rostworowski, *History of the Inca Realm*, pp. 5–6.
13. Luis G. Lumbreras, *The Peoples and Cultures of Ancient Peru*, trans. Betty J. Meggers. Washington, DC: Smithsonian Institution Press, 1974, p. 162.

Chapter 2: The Rise of the Incas

14. Morris and von Hagen, *The Inka Empire and Its Andean Origins*, p. 148.
15. Quoted in Laura Laurencich Minelli, ed., *The Inca World: The Development of Pre-Columbian Peru,* A.D. *1000–1534*. Norman: University of Oklahoma Press, 1999, p. 135.
16. Fagan, *Kingdoms of Gold, Kingdoms of Jade*, p. 42.
17. Garcilaso de la Vega, *Royal Commentaries of the Incas and General History of Peru*. 2 vols., trans. Harold V. Livermore. Austin: University of Texas Press, 1966, p. 280.
18. Fagan, *Kingdoms of Gold, Kingdoms of Jade*, p. 197.
19. Moseley, *The Incas and Their Ancestors*, p. 15.
20. Bernabe Cobo, *History of the Inca Empire*, ed. and trans. Roland Hamilton.

Austin: University of Texas Press, 1979, p. 143.

21. Nigel Davies, *The Incas*. Niwot: University Press of Colorado, 1995, p. 12.

Chapter 3: Emperors, Aristocrats, and Commoners

22. Moseley, *The Incas and Their Ancestors*, p. 53.
23. Rostworowski, *History of the Inca Realm*, pp. 15–16.
24. Kendall, *Everyday Life of the Incas*, p. 65.
25. Davies, *The Incas*, p. 114.
26. Quoted in Kendall, *Everyday Life of the Incas*, p. 77.
27. Lanning, *Peru Before the Incas*, p. 161.
28. Malpass, *Daily Life in the Inca Empire*, pp. 79–80.

Chapter 4: Bureaucrats and Taxpayers

29. Quoted in Minelli, ed., *The Inca World: The Development of Pre-Columbian Peru*, p. 180.
30. Louis Baudin, *Daily Life in Peru Under the Last Incas*, trans. Winifred Bradford. New York: Macmillan, 1961, p. 223.
31. Craig Morris and Donald E. Thompson, *Huánuco Pampa: An Inca City and Its Hinterlands*. London: Thames and Hudson, 1985, pp. 93–94.
32. Morris and von Hagen, *The Inka Empire and Its Andean Origins*, p. 114.
33. Rebecca Stone-Miller, *Art of the Andes: From Chavín to Inca*. London: Thames and Hudson, 1995, p. 196.
34. Quoted in Minelli, ed., *The Inca World*, p. 190.
35. George Bankes, *Peru Before Pizarro*. Oxford: Phaidon Press, 1977, p. 117.
36. Morris and von Hagen, *The Inka Empire and Its Andean Origins*, p. 171.

Chapter 5: Gods and Priests

37. Baudin, *Daily Life in Peru Under the Last Incas*, p. 67.
38. Constance Classen, *Inca Cosmology and the Human Body*. Salt Lake City: University of Utah Press, 1993, p. 125.
39. Fagan, *Kingdoms of Gold, Kingdoms of Jade*, p. 48.
40. Michael Coe, Dean Snow, and Elizabeth Benson, *Atlas of Ancient America*. New York: Facts On File, 1986, p. 198.
41. Kendall, *Everyday Life of the Incas*, p. 192.
42. Bankes, *Peru Before Pizarro*, pp. 153–54.
43. Quoted in George A. Collier, Renato I. Rosaldo, and John D. Wirth, eds., *The Inca and Aztec States, 1400–1800: Anthropology and History*. New York: Academic Press, 1982, pp. 109–10.
44. John Hyslop, *Inka Settlement Planning*. Austin: University of Texas Press, 1990, p. 148.

Chapter 6: Soldiers and Engineers

45. Davies, *The Incas*, p. 148.
46. Baudin, *Daily Life in Peru Under the Last Incas*, pp. 132–33.
47. Juan de Betanzos, *Narrative of the Incas*, ed. and trans. Roland Hamilton and Dana Buchanan. Austin: University of Texas Press, 1996, p. 147.
48. John Hyslop, *The Inka Road System*. Orlando, FL: Academic Press, 1984, p. 2.

49. Quoted in Morris and Thompson, *Huánuco Pampa*, p. 89.
50. Bankes, *Peru Before Pizarro*, p. 193.
51. Kenneth R. Wright and Alfredo Valencia Zegarra, *Machu Picchu: A Civil Engineering Marvel*. Reston, VA: American Society of Civil Engineers, 2000, p. 1.
52. Quoted in Paul G. Bahn, ed., *Lost Cities*. New York: Welcome Rain, 1997, p. 197.

Chapter 7: The Fall of the Incas

53. Edward Hyams and George Ordish, *The Last of the Incas*. London: Longmans, 1963, p. 145.
54. James Lockhart, *The Men of Cajamarca: A Social and Biographical Study of the First Conquerors of Peru*. Austin: University of Texas Press, 1972, p. 140.
55. Rostworowski, *History of the Inca Realm*, p. 67.
56. Quoted in Jared Diamond, *Guns, Germs, and Steel: The Fates of Human Societies*. New York: Norton, 1997, p. 69.
57. Albert Marrin, *Inca and Spaniard: Pizarro and the Conquest of Peru*. New York: Atheneum, 1989, p. 81.
58. Samuel K. Lothrop, *Inca Treasure as Depicted by Spanish Historians*. Los Angeles: Southwest Museum, 1938, p. 52.
59. Hyams and Ordish, *The Last of the Incas*, p. 234.
60. Diamond, *Guns, Germs, and Steel*, p. 77.

Epilogue: The Incan Legacy

61. Stone-Miller, *Art of the Andes: From Chavín to Inca*, p. 218.
62. Malpass, *Daily Life in the Inca Empire*, pp. xxviii–xxix.

For Further Reading

Books

Daniele Kuss, *Incas*. New York: Marshall Cavendish, 1991. Filled with color illustrations, this retelling of Incan myths and legends also includes a useful discussion of the imperial religion.

Peter Lourie, *Lost Treasure of the Inca*. Honesdale, PA: Boyds Mills Press, 1999. Describes the adventures of the author in his recent search for the lost treasure of the Incas. Color photographs of Incan gold jewelry and figures and a historical narrative link the present to the past.

Fiona MacDonald, *Inca Town*. New York: Franklin Watts, 1999. Skillfully uses color drawings and cutaways of temples, homes, and workshops to describe the everyday life of the Incas.

Elizabeth Mann, *Machu Picchu: The Story of the Amazing Inkas and Their City in the Clouds*. New York: Mikaya Press, 2000. Presents the history of Machu Picchu, detailing the Incas' building and use of the city. Full-page color illustrations, photographs, and maps supplement the text.

Hazel Mary Martell, *Civilizations of Peru Before 1535*. Austin, TX: Raintree Steck-Vaughn, 1999. Illustrations and maps help tell the stories of several ancient Peruvian civilizations, including the Incas, and the impact of the Spanish conquest on these people.

Marion Morrison, *Atahuallpa and the Incas*. New York: Bookwright, 1986. A useful biography of the Incan emperor Atahuallpa, making use of illustrations and maps to detail the last Incan civil war and the Spanish conquest.

———, *An Inca Farmer*. Vero Beach, FL: Rourke Enterprises, 1988. Describes the life of an Incan farmer during the height of the empire.

Dennis Nishi, *The Inca Empire*. San Diego: Lucent Books, 2000. Filled with instructive illustrations, this book traces the rise and fall of the Inca Empire. It contains excerpts from period documents, maps, a time line, and a reading list.

Matti A. Pitkanen, *The Grandchildren of the Incas*. Minneapolis: Carolrhoda Books, 1991. Contrasts and compares the life of the present-day Quechua Indians of Peru with their Incan ancestors. Color photographs of the modern people capture the reality of their lives and homeland.

Johan Reinhard, *Discovering the Inca Ice Maiden: My Adventures on Ampato*. Washington, DC: National Geographic Society, 1998. A first-hand report of the 1995 discovery and study of the mummy of a young Incan girl found on the Peruvian volcano Mount Ampato. Along with the text are color photographs of the mummy and its artifacts.

Timothy R. Roberts, *Gods of the Maya, Aztecs, and Incas*. New York: MetroBooks, 1996. Examines the beliefs and religious practices of the Incas, showing the effect of religion on everyday life and moral codes.

Philip Steele, *The Incas and Machu Picchu*. New York: Dillon Press, 1993. Describes Hiram Bingham's 1911 expedition that found Machu Picchu. Maps and illustrations, many in color, help fill out the account.

Tim Wood, *The Incas*. New York: Viking, 1996. Using double-page, peel-away transparencies, this work allows readers to look inside an Inca house, a temple, a palace, and a roadside way station.

Richard Worth, *Pizarro and the Conquest of the Incan Empire in World History*. Berkeley Heights, NJ: Enslow Publishers, 2000. Tells the story of the Spanish conquest of the Incas. Period documents, illustrations, and maps help in unfolding the complex tale.

Websites

The Incas: A Pictorial Tribute to Their Art and Culture, 1997 (www.theincas.com). Contains excellent color images of Incan stonework, pottery, and gold jewelry.

Incas and Conquistadors, 2000 (www.westering.dial.pipex.com/incas/home.shtml#top). Provides useful information on many Incan rulers and Incan cities, the latter accompanied by photographs. Also has a reading list and links to other Incan history sites.

Lost Cities Adventures, 1998 (www.destination360.com/lostcities.htm). Holds color photographs of the ruins at Machu Picchu and other Incan sites in Peru.

Teacher Oz's Kingdom of History, 2001 (members.aol.com/Tchrfromoz/frames.html). An excellent site that has useful links to maps, the history of the Inca Empire, achievements of the Incas, an account of the Spanish conquest, Incan descendants, and Machu Picchu.

Works Consulted

Abraham Arias-Larreta, *Pre-Columbian Literatures: Aztec—Incan—Maya-Quiché*. Book 1: *History of Indoamerican Literature*. Los Angeles: New World Library, 1964. Contains a useful discussion of Incan poetry, along with examples.

Paul G. Bahn, ed., *The Cambridge Illustrated History of Archaeology*. Cambridge, England: Cambridge University Press, 1996. An encyclopedic history of archaeology, from its beginnings to the present.

———, *Lost Cities*. New York: Welcome Rain, 1997. A collection of illustrated articles, written by archaeologists, describing some fifty ancient cities, among them the pre-Incan Tiwanaku and the Incan Machu Picchu.

George Bankes, *Peru Before Pizarro*. Oxford: Phaidon Press, 1977. Looks at the social structures, governments, religious practices, and crafts of the Incas and their predecessors.

Louis Baudin, *Daily Life in Peru Under the Last Incas*. Trans. Winifred Bradford. New York: Macmillan, 1961. A noted Incan scholar paints a vivid picture of the public and private lives of the Incan nobility, bureaucrats, soldiers, priests, farmers, and artisans.

Hans Bauman, *Gold and Gods of Peru*. Trans. Stella Humphries. New York: Pantheon Books, 1963. A history of Peruvian archaeology.

Stephen Bertman, *Doorways Through Time: The Romance of Archaeology*. Los Angeles: Tarcher, 1986. A concise, knowledgeable history of archaeology.

Juan de Betanzos, *Narrative of the Incas*. Ed. and trans. Roland Hamilton and Dana Buchanan. Austin: University of Texas Press, 1996. A sixteenth-century chronicle of the Inca Empire and the Spanish conquest. The author, fluent in Quechua, the Inca language, interviewed many Incas, particularly those related to the old ruling family.

John Bierhorst, ed. and trans., *Black Rainbow: Legends of the Incas and Myths of Ancient Peru*. New York: Farrar, Straus and Giroux,

1976. A collection of Incan legends and myths, originally collected by various Spanish writers.

Alfred M. Bingham, *Portrait of an Explorer: Hiram Bingham, Discoverer of Machu Picchu*. Ames: University of Iowa Press, 1989. A well-researched biography of the twentieth-century discoverer of Machu Picchu.

Pedro de Cieza de León, *Discovery and Conquest of Peru: Chronicles of the New World Encounter*. Ed. and trans. Alexandra Parma Cook and Noble David Cook. Durham, NC: Duke University Press, 1998. This exhaustive chronicle of the Spanish conquest of the Inca Empire is judged by historians as the best and most reliable of the contemporary accounts. Its author was a soldier who served in Peru for several years, beginning in 1547.

———, *The Incas*. Ed. Victor Wolfgang von Hagen. Trans. Harriet de Onis. Norman: University of Oklahoma Press, 1959. Selections from one of the most important early writings about the Incas, their history, and their society.

Constance Classen, *Inca Cosmology and the Human Body*. Salt Lake City: University of Utah Press, 1993. Describes Incan religious beliefs and practices, explaining how they affected Incan society.

Bernabe Cobo, *History of the Inca Empire*. Ed. and trans. Roland Hamilton. Austin: University of Texas Press, 1979. Selections from a classic seventeenth-century history of the Inca Empire, written by a Spanish Jesuit who spent most of his adult life in Peru.

Michael Coe, Dean Snow, and Elizabeth Benson, *Atlas of Ancient America*. New York: Facts On File, 1986. Filled with illustrations and maps, the sections on Andean cultures are packed with valuable information.

George A. Collier, Renato I. Rosaldo, and John D. Wirth, eds., *The Inca and Aztec States, 1400–1800: Anthropology and History*. New York: Academic Press, 1982. Included in this collection are a number of scholarly essays discussing how the Incas administered their empire.

Terence N. D'Altroy, *Provincial Power in the Inka Empire*. Washington, DC: Smithsonian Institution Press, 1992. Based on the author's own fieldwork, this study examines Incan political and military strategies used to control imperial provinces.

Nigel Davies, *The Incas*. Niwot: University Press of Colorado, 1995. A working archaeologist presents a good overview of the rise and fall of the Inca Empire.

Jared Diamond, *Guns, Germs, and Steel: The Fates of Human Societies*. New York: Norton, 1997. A study of the factors leading to conquest, with a detailed analysis of the fall of the Inca Empire.

David Ewing Duncan, *Hernando de Soto: A Savage Quest in the Americas*. New York: Crown, 1995. Impressive research combines with good writing to tell the story of one of the conquistadors who helped overthrow the Inca Empire.

Brian M. Fagan, *Kingdoms of Gold, Kingdoms of Jade: The Americas Before Columbus*. London: Thames and Hudson, 1991. In concise, fact-filled chapters, a distinguished anthropologist covers the Inca Empire and its predecessors, along with other cultures of the Americas.

Brian M. Fagan, ed., *Eyewitness to Discovery: First-Person Accounts of More Than Fifty of the World's Greatest Archaeological Discoveries*. Oxford: Oxford University Press, 1996. A fascinating compilation of archaeologists writing about their most important discoveries.

Rafael Varón Gabai, *Francisco Pizarro and His Brothers: The Illusion of Power in Sixteenth-Century Peru*. Trans. Javier Flores Espinoza. Norman: University of Oklahoma Press, 1997. Looks at the struggle for power of the Pizarro brothers during and after the conquest of the Incas.

Garcilaso de la Vega, *Royal Commentaries of the Incas and General History of Peru*. 2 vols. Trans. Harold V. Livermore. Austin: University of Texas Press, 1966. This thorough sixteenth-century study is an important early history of the Inca Empire. The author was part Inca, his mother being a cousin to the last Incan ruler.

The Huarochirí Manuscript: A Testament of Ancient and Colonial Andean Religion. Trans. Frank Salomon and George L. Urioste. Austin: University of Texas Press, 1991. A seventeenth-century document that reproduces the religious stories of non-Incan Andeans. Several of the sections are secular, showing how other ethnic groups within the Inca Empire viewed the Incas and their administrative practices.

Edward Hyams and George Ordish, *The Last of the Incas*. London: Longmans, 1963. A probing look at the final years of the Inca

Empire and the internal conflicts and problems that led up to its conquest by the Spanish.

John Hyslop, *The Inka Road System*. Orlando, FL: Academic Press, 1984. An eminent archaeologist discusses in detail Incan roads, where they ran, how many there were, how many miles they covered, and how they were built.

———, *Inka Settlement Planning*. Austin: University of Texas Press, 1990. A comprehensive survey of Incan urban planning as revealed through archaeological studies of a number of Incan cities.

Federico Kauffmann-Doig, *Ancestors of the Incas: The Lost Civilizations of Peru*. Trans. Eulogio Guzmán. Memphis, TN: Wonders, 1998. With the aid of beautiful color plates, many full-paged, this study conveys the richness of pre-Incan textiles, pottery, and gold work.

Ann Kendall, *Everyday Life of the Incas*. London: B.T. Batsford, 1973. A study by a distinguished scholar of all aspects of Incan society, from public to private, shows what life was like in the capital and in the provinces.

Edward P. Lanning, *Peru Before the Incas*. Englewood Cliffs, NJ: Prentice-Hall, 1967. A study of the history and customs of ancient Peruvian cultures that, despite its title, includes the Incas.

James Lockhart, *The Men of Cajamarca: A Social and Biographical Study of the First Conquerors of Peru*. Austin: University of Texas Press, 1972. A series of short but informative biographies of many of the Spaniards who took part in the conquest of the Inca Empire.

Samuel K. Lothrop, *Inca Treasure as Depicted by Spanish Historians*. Los Angeles: Southwest Museum, 1938. Discusses Incan treasures described by the Spanish, as well as Incan mining operations and gold crafting.

Luis G. Lumbreras, *The Peoples and Cultures of Ancient Peru*. Trans. Betty J. Meggers. Washington, DC: Smithsonian Institution Press, 1974. A Peruvian archaeologist's history of the pre-Incan cultures of Peru.

Michael A. Malpass, *Daily Life in the Inca Empire*. Westport, CT: Greenwood Press, 1996. This prominent archaeologist first traces the history of the pre-Incas and the Incas and then discusses many aspects of Incan society, such as politics, private lives, and religion.

Michael A. Malpass, ed., *Provincial Inca: Archaeological and Ethnohistorical Assessment of the Impact of the Inca State*. Iowa City: University of Iowa Press, 1993. Scholarly articles examining occupation, control, and administration of the provinces by the Inca Empire.

Clements R. Markham, ed. and trans., *Narratives of the Rites and Laws of the Yncas*. New York: Burt Franklin, 1873. Dating from the sixteenth and seventeenth centuries, these four Spanish colonial documents describe Incan laws, customs, religion, and history. One is written by a native Andean.

Albert Marrin, *Inca and Spaniard: Pizarro and the Conquest of Peru*. New York: Atheneum, 1989. A good modern history of the Spanish conquest of the Incas.

Francesco Menotti, *The Inkas: Last Stage of Stone Masonry Development in the Andes*. Oxford: Archaeopress, 1998. Explains how the Incas worked stone to use it to build their cities.

Laura Laurencich Minelli, ed., *The Inca World: The Development of Pre-Columbian Peru, A.D. 1000–1534*. Norman: University of Oklahoma Press, 1999. Nicely illustrated with maps and color plates, this collection of essays by Andean scholars traces the rise and fall of the pre-Spanish cultures of Peru.

Fernando Montesinos, *Memorias Antiguas Historiales del Peru (Report of the Ancient History of Peru)*. Ed. and trans. Philip Ainsworth Means. Nendeln, Liechtenstein: Kraus, 1920. The author, a seventeenth-century Jesuit who spent several years in Peru, provides worthwhile information about Incan cultures, despite a number of inaccuracies.

Craig Morris and Donald E. Thompson, *Huánuco Pampa: An Inca City and Its Hinterlands*. London: Thames and Hudson, 1985. An informative study of life in an Incan provincial town as uncovered by two archaeologists who excavated there.

Craig Morris and Adriana von Hagen, *The Inka Empire and Its Andean Origins*. New York: Abbeville Press, 1993. Color photographs enhance this clearly written study of the history and customs of pre-Incas and Incas.

Michael E. Moseley, *The Incas and Their Ancestors: The Archaeology of Peru*. London: Thames and Hudson, 1992. A prominent scholar's detailed history of the Incas and other Andean cultures.

Susan A. Niles, *Callachaca: Style and Status in an Inca Community*. Iowa City: University of Iowa Press, 1987. A leading expert on Incan royal estates discusses her findings at one such site.

William H. Prescott, *History of the Conquest of Peru*. New York: Heritage Press, 1847. A classic history of the Spanish conquest of the Inca Empire.

Colin Renfrew and Paul Bahn, *Archaeology: Theories, Methods, and Practices*. London: Thames and Hudson, 1991. A complete introduction to archaeology, explaining what archaeologists do, why they do it, and how they do it.

María Rostworowski de Diez Canseco, *History of the Inca Realm*. Trans. Harry B. Iceland. Cambridge, England: Cambridge University Press, 1999. A celebrated Incan historian makes extensive use of original manuscripts of Spanish chronicles and colonial records to present the history of the Incas and to detail the workings of their society.

John Howland Rowe and Dorothy Menzel, eds., *Peruvian Archaeology: Selected Readings*. Palo Alto, CA: Peek Publications, 1967. A collection of essays by distinguished archaeologists discussing their findings about pre-Incan and Incan culture.

Stuart Stirling, *The Last Conquistador: Mansio Serra de Leguizamón and the Conquest of the Incas*. Thrupp, UK: Sutton Publishing, 1999. A short history of the Spanish conquest of the Incas, accompanied by the memoir of the conquistador Mansio Serra de Leguizamón.

Rebecca Stone-Miller, *Art of the Andes: From Chavín to Inca*. London: Thames and Hudson, 1995. Art historian's well-illustrated examination of the arts and crafts of several Andean cultures, ending with the Incas.

Gary Urton, *The History of a Myth: Pacariqtambo and the Origin of the Inkas*. Austin: University of Texas Press, 1990. Examines the relationship between Incan myth and history.

Kenneth R. Wright and Alfredo Valencia Zegarra, *Machu Picchu: A Civil Engineering Marvel*. Reston, VA: American Society of Civil Engineers, 2000. An experienced civil engineer and an eminent Peruvian archaeologist describe the construction of Machu Picchu in this thorough, well-illustrated study.

INDEX

Account of the Conquest of Peru, An (Sancho), 41
accountants, 52–54
acllas. *See* Chosen Women
afterlife, 58–59, 63
agriculture, 12–14, 40–41, 91–92
  of early Incas, 24
  farmers as soldiers, 69–70
  of Huari society, 22
  program of Pachucuti Inca Yupanqui, 30
  taxation and, 47–48
  types of crops, 45
alpacas, 13–14, 46, 92
Amazon River, 24
Ampato (volcano), 63–64
Andes mountains, 6, 12, 63, 64, 72–74
animals. *See* alpacas; food supply; guinea pigs; llamas
apos (prefects), 48
archaeology, 9–10
architecture, 91
  of bridges, 74–75
  of Chan Chan, 29
  of Chimú society, 27
  of cities, 76–78
  of military posts, 68
  of roads, 72–74
  of Tiwanaku society, 20
Argentina, 7, 72
aristocracy. *See* nobility
armor, 71, 84–85
army. *See* military
art, 15–17, 91
Art of the Andes (Stone-Miller), 16
artifacts. *See* jewelry; pottery; textiles; tools
Atahuallpa (emperor)
  ambitions for throne, 80–81
  conquered by Spaniards, 84–88
  death of, 86–88
ayllus, 34–35
  livestock of, 46
  modern-day, 92

Bahn, Paul G., 29
bartering. *See* reciprocity
Baudin, Louis, 64
Betanzos, Juan de, 72
Bolivia, 7, 12
boys
  chosen for priesthood, 60
  coming of age rituals for, 38, 39
  education of, 47
  sacrifice of, 62–63
bridges, 74–75
buildings. *See* architecture
burial
  afterlife and, 58
  mummies, 58, 60, 65
  of sacrifices, 63
  tombs, 10, 29

Cabello de Balboa, Miguel, 23
Cahuachi (city), 18
Cajamarca (city), 82, 84–86
Calca (town), 26
calendar, 64–65
canals, 27
cannibalism, 31
Capac Raymi (festival), 92
Caral society, 14–15
Catholicism, 92
cavalry, 85, 87, 90
Chan Chan, 27, 29
Chanca society, 9, 25–27, 88
Chavín de Huantar (village), 15
Chavín movement, 15

chicha (corn beer), 45, 54, 61–62, 92
Chile, 7, 72
Chimú society, 27, 29
Chosen Women, 54–55, 61–62
Christianity, 89, 92
Cieza de León, Pedro de, 9, 76, 82
  on Coricancha, 59
  on corn harvest, 61
  on Cuzco, 26, 88
  on Tiwanaku, 20
cities, 14, 48, 76–79
  see also individual city names
class structure, 34
  afterlife and, 59
  commoners, 40–43, 52, 59, 67, 76
  curacas, 39, 51, 67, 70, 75
  lifestyle of emperors, 36–38
  military and, 67–68
  nobility, 38–39, 43, 52, 59, 67
  see also ayllus; emperors
climate, 12, 57, 63
clothing, 36, 41–43, 48, 55, 63–64
  cotton, 12, 45
  of Moche society, 18
  of nobility, 39
  textiles, 16, 19, 27–28, 55, 91
  wool, 46
  worn by soldiers, 70, 71
  see also armor
coastal lowlands, 12, 74–75
Cobo, Bernabe, 31–32, 37, 43, 50, 73
Colla society, 25–27, 31
Colombia, 7
commoners, 76
  afterlife for, 59
  in military, 67
  tax exemptions for, 52
  see also mit'a system
Coricancha (Temple of the Sun), 59–60
corn, 22, 45, 49, 60–61, 91
Corpus Christi (festival), 92
cotton, 12, 45
  see also textiles
coyas (empresses), 35
crafts, 15–17
cults, 15
curacas (non-Incan officials), 75
  in military, 67, 70
  roles of, 39, 51
  senior, 82
Cuzco (city), 6
  architecture of, 30, 76–78
  Battle of, 25–26
  Coricancha, 59–60
  divisions of, 48
  Spaniards in, 88–90
Cuzco Valley, 21

Daily Life in Peru Under the Last Incas (Baudin), 64
deserts, 12
Diamond, Jared, 87
Discovery and Conquest of Peru (Cieza de León), 82, 88
disease, 80

Earth God (Pacha-Mama), 57, 92
earthquakes, 12, 57, 91, 92
economy
  Chosen Women and, 55
  money introduced by Spaniards, 90
  reciprocity, 44, 46
Ecuador, 7, 72, 80, 89
education, 39, 40, 47, 55
emperors, 7
  in battle, 70
  as descendants from Inti, 56
  household of, 35–36
  land of, 44–45
  Sapa Inca designation, 36
  succession of, 37–38, 62
  see also individual emperor names
empresses, 43
engineering, 14
  see also architecture
European Renaissance, 91
Everyday Life of the Incas (Kendall), 41
execution, 51, 63, 72

fasting, 65
food supply
  animals for, 13–14, 46, 92
  chicha, 45, 54, 61–62, 92
  corn, 22, 45, 49, 60–61, 91
  increased with agricultural plan, 30
  see also agriculture; religion

gender roles, 34–35, 41–43
see also boys; girls; women
geoglyphs, 17
geography
  difficulty of, 12
  of Tahuantinsuyu, 6–7
  as taught to boys, 47
  terraces, 21–22
  see also bridges; roads
girls
  as Chosen Women, 55
  sacrifice of, 62–63
gods, 30
gold, 46, 83, 86, 89, 91
gourds, 45
government, 48–53
  see also curacas; emperors; *mit'a* system
Guardian of Ten/Fifty, 67
guinea pigs, 13–14, 92
Guns, Germs, and Steel (Diamond), 87

headdresses, 18, 36, 39, 64, 70
  see also helmets
heaven, 59
hell, 59
helmets, 71
highlands. *See* mountains
History of Peru (Cabello de Balboa), 23
History of the Inca Empire (Cobo), 31–32, 37, 43, 50, 73
horses, 85, 87, 90
households. *See* ayllus
huacas (spirits), 58, 66, 70, 92
Huánuco Pampa (city), 46, 49, 54
Huánuco Pampa (Morris and Thompson), 49, 54
Huari society, 19–22

Huascar (emperor), 80–81, 86
Huayna Capac (emperor), 32, 80
Huayna Capac (mine), 41
human sacrifice, 32
Hyslop, John, 68

Illapa, the Thunder God, 56–57, 62
Inca (title for emperors), 7
Incas
  conquered by Spaniards, 82–89
  ethnic composition of, 7–8
  legacy of, 91–92
  resisted Spaniards, 89–90
  settled in Cuzco Valley, 23–24
  War of the Two Brothers, 80–81, 83, 86
  wealth of, 46, 83, 86, 89, 91
  see also agriculture; architecture; class structure; clothing; emperors; gender roles; wars
Incas, The (Cieza de León), 20, 26, 59, 61
Incas-by-blood, 38–39
Incas-by-privilege, 37–38
Inca Urcon (emperor), 25, 26
Inca Yupanqui. *See* Pachacuti Inca Yupanqui; Topa Inca Yupanqui
incest, 35, 37
Inka Settlement Planning (Hyslop), 68
inns, 75, 84
Inti, the Sun God, 56–57, 62
irrigation, 14, 45

jewelry, 46, 58, 64
  see also gold; silver

Kendall, Ann, 41

labor force, 14–15, 32, 40
  see also mit'a system
Lake Titicaca
  culture of, 11, 19
  under Inca rule, 27
  religious significance of, 56
land, 44–45
Land of the Four Quarters. *See* Tahuantinsuyu
language. *See* Quechua language

legal system, 50
  see also punishment
Lima, Peru, 90
livestock, 13–14
llamas, 13–14, 46, 92
  for battle, 70
  sacrifice of, 46, 61–62, 65–66
  for transport, 72
Locke, Leland L., 54
Lost Cities (Bahn), 29
Lumbreras, Luis G., 18
Lupaca society, 25, 31

Machu Picchu, 6
  archaelogical discoveries at, 10
  design of, 30, 77, 79
  roads to, 74
Machu Picchu: A Civil Engineering Marvel (Wright and Zegarra), 77
maize. *See* corn
Mama-Cocha, the Sea God, 57
Mama-Quilla, the Moon God, 56–57
mamaconas. *See* Chosen Women
Manco Capac (emperor), 23, 35, 36
Manco Inca (emperor), 89–90
marriage, 34–35, 39
masonry, 76–77
mathematics, 14, 47
medicine, 17–18
messengers, 75
military
  campaigns against Chimú, 27–28
  control of coast, 29
  horses, 85, 87, 90
  of Huari, 21
  organization of, 67–69
  preparation for war, 70–72
  punishment for defeated chiefs, 31–32, 72
  raids by early Incas, 24
  roads for, 67, 72–74
  training of, 39
  treatment of conquered societies, 56
mines, 41, 46
mit'a system, 47–48
  maintained by Spaniards, 90
  in military, 67, 69
  resettlement and, 52
Moche society, 18–19
money, 90
  see also economy
monuments, 20
Moon God. *See* Mama-Quilla
Morris, Craig, 46, 49, 54
mountains, 6, 12, 63, 64, 72–74
mummies, 58, 60, 65
music, 47, 70

natural disasters. *See* earthquakes; volcanoes
Nazca society, 17–18
Necropolis, 17
Nevado Ampato (volcano), 63, 64
Ninan Cuyuchi, 80
nobility
  afterlife for, 59
  lifestyle of, 39–40
  in military, 67
  tax exemptions for, 52
  women of, 43

Pacha-Mama, the Earth God, 57, 92
Pachacuti Inca Yupanqui (emperor), 9, 20, 25–29
  agricultural program of, 30
  Cuzco designed by, 78
  divine nature of, 56
  wife of, 43
Pambamarca (military post), 68
Paracas society, 17–18
Peoples and Cultures of Ancient Peru (Lumbreras), 18
Peru, 7, 14, 63, 72, 89–90
Pichu Pichu (mountain), 63, 64
Pizarro, Francisco, 82–85
  capture of Atahuallpa, 86–88
  resisted by Incans, 89–90
plateaus, 12
polygamy, 35
  see also marriage

population
  ethnic composition of, 7–8
  of modern-day South America, 10
  non-Incan, 56
    see also curacas
  in 1300s, 24
  see also class structure
potatoes, 45, 49, 91
pottery, 91
  of Chimú society, 27–28
  found in storehouses, 49
  of Huari society, 21
  manufacturing of, 48
  of Moche society, 18
  of Tiwanaku society, 19, 21
prefects. *See apos*
Prescott, William H., 11, 19
priestesses, 60
priesthood, 39, 60–61
prisoners of war, 72
punishment, 31–32, 50, 51, 62, 72

Quechua language, 10, 51, 91, 92
  spoken by modern-day South Americans, 10
  spoken by Spaniards, 90
quipucamayocs (accountants), 52–54
quipus, 53, 75
Quito (city), 32

rain forests, 30–31
reciprocity, 44, 46
  see also economy
records, historical, 8–9, 23
  see also archaeology
Reinhard, Johan, 63
religion, 27–28, 30, 48
  afterlife, 58–59
  burial customs, 10, 29, 58, 60, 65
  of conquered societies, 52
  cults, 15
  gods, 56–59
  Machu Picchu as retreat, 79
  modern-day, 92
  portrayal of, 9
  replaced by Christianity, 89
  sacrifice and, 31–32, 46, 61–66, 72
  spirit world, 58
resettlement, 52, 69
rivers, 14, 24
roads, 67
  built by Huari society, 22
  for military, 67, 72–74
  Spaniards' impressions of, 84
  as symbols of authority, 76
rocks
  fine masonry, 76–77
  sacred, 58
Royal Commentaries of the Incas (Vega), 25, 38, 42, 47
royalty. *See* emperors; *individual emperor names*
Ruiz de Arce, Juan, 84

sacrifice ceremonies
  animal, 46, 61, 62, 65–66
  human, 31–32, 62–65, 72
  see also religion
Sacsahuaman (wall structure), 76, 90
San Pedro Cacha (city), 59–60
Sancho, Pedro, 41
sanitation, 43
Sapa Inca, 36
  divine nature of, 56–57
  gifts to military officers from, 72
  see also emperors; *individual emperor names*
Sayri Topa (Manco Inca's son), 90
Sea God. *See* Mama-Cocha
servants, 39, 43, 52
sexual activity, 62
Shady Solís, Ruth, 14
silver, 46, 86, 89, 91
sky gods, 56–57
slavery, 18
Spaniards
  conquistadors, 6, 82–88
  language used by, 51, 91
  records of, 8–9, 23
  resisted by Incans, 89–90
  see also individual names of Spaniards

spirit world, 58, 92
statues, 56
Stone-Miller, Rebecca, 16
stones. *See* rocks
storehouses, 49
Sun
  divine link to emperors, 36
  Inti, the Sun God, 56–57
  temples of the, 19, 30, 59–60
Sun God. *See* Inti
Supé River Valley, 14

taclla (foot plow), 40–41
Tahuantinsuyu *(Tawantinsuyu)*, 6–7
tambos. *See* inns
taxes, 46–48, 52
  see also mit'a system
Tello, Julio, 11, 15, 17
temples, 19, 30, 59–60
terraces, 21–22, 30
textiles, 91
  of Chimú society, 27–28
  Karawa, 16
  of Tiwanaku society, 19
  weaving of, 42, 55
Thompson, Donald E., 46, 49, 54
thrones, 36, 60
Thunder God. *See* Illapa
Tiwanaku society, 19–20, 22
tocricoc apos (provincial governors), 48
tombs, 10, 29
  see also burial
tools, 12, 40–41, 46
Topa Amaru (emperor), 90, 91
Topa Huallpa (Atahuallpa's brother), 88
Topa Inca Yupanqui, 27–29, 56, 72
  death of, 32
  military campaign in rain forest, 30–31
torture, 51
  see also punishment
travel, 67, 72–75
Trujillo, Diego de, 87

Uhle, Max, 11, 19
Urubamba River, 24

Vega, Garcilaso de la, 76
  on Viracocha Inca, 9
Viracocha (god), 56, 62
Viracocha Inca (emperor), 9, 24–25, 56
Virgins of the Sun, 61–62
  see also Chosen Women
volcanoes, 63, 92

Wari. *See* Huari society
wars
  Battle of Cuzco, 25–26
  ceremonies for, 66
  preparation for, 70–72
  between Spaniards and Incans, 86–88
  War of the Two Brothers, 80–81, 83, 86
  see also military
water
  canals, 27
  irrigation, 14, 45
  Mama-Cocha and, 57
  rivers, 14, 24
wealth. *see* class structure; gold; silver
weapons, 71, 84–85
weather, 12, 57, 63
weaving, 42, 55
Wise, Karen, 29
women
  Chosen Women, 54–55, 61–62
  of commoner class, 41–43
  as "gifts," 72
  of noble class, 43
  portrayed as gods, 57
  priestesses, 60
  tax obligations of, 48
wool, 46
  see also textiles
Wright, Kenneth R., 77

yanaconas. *See* servants

Zegarra, Alfredo Valencia, 77

Picture Credits

Cover Photo: PhotoDisc

© Archivo Iconographico, S.A./CORBIS, 8

© Nathan Benn/ CORBIS, 19

© Bettmann/ CORBIS, 25

© Bowers Museum of Cultural Art/ CORBIS, 17, 42, 46

© Pablo Corral V/ CORBIS, 13

© Leonard de Selva/ CORBIS, 44

© Owen Franken/CORBIS, 92

© Jeremy Horner/ CORBIS, 21

Hulton/Archive by Getty Images, 57, 58, 65, 78, 84

© Wolfgang Kaehler/ CORBIS, 45

© Kea Publishing Services Ltd./ CORBIS, 49

© Charles & Josette Lenars/ CORBIS, 63

© Francis G Mayer/ CORBIS, 9

© Michael Nicholson/ CORBIS, 11

North Wind Picture Archives, 27, 28, 31, 32, 35, 60, 67, 71, 74, 75, 81, 87, 89

© Chris Rainier/CORBIS, 7

© Galen Rowell/ CORBIS, 14

© Kevin Schafer/ CORBIS, 20

Stock Montage, Inc., 40, 53, 85

© Brian Vikander/ CORBIS, 69

About the Author

James A. Corrick has been a professional writer and editor for twenty years and is the author of twenty-five books, as well as two hundred articles and short stories. Other books for Lucent are *The Early Middle Ages*, *The Late Middle Ages*, *The Battle of Gettysburg*, *The Byzantine Empire*, *The Renaissance*, *The Industrial Revolution*, *The Civil War: Life Among the Soldiers and Cavalry*, *The Louisiana Purchase*, and *Life of a Medieval Knight*. Along with a Ph.D. in English, Corrick's academic background includes a graduate degree in the biological sciences. He has taught English, tutored minority students, edited magazines for the National Space Society, been a science writer for the Muscular Dystrophy Association, and edited and indexed books on history, economics, and literature for Columbia University Press, MIT Press, and others. He and his wife live in Tucson, Arizona.